Dough oops Do

A very indulge...

I hope you don't rip your
hair out at the grammatical
errors.

Lots of love.

Tockley

XXX

Guys, Goats and Organic Farming

ESTELLE CURWEN

authorHOUSE®

AuthorHouse™ UK
1663 Liberty Drive
Bloomington, IN 47403 USA
www.authorhouse.co.uk
Phone: 0800.197.4150

Published by AuthorHouse 12/07/2016

ISBN: 978-1-5246-6671-2 (sc)
ISBN: 978-1-5246-6672-9 (hc)
ISBN: 978-1-5246-6670-5 (e)

Contents

October 2004

London (my favourite place) where there are too many of the wrong kind of people, too many buildings not enough trees, noise rather than nature's musical tune. And yet where I find myself today, alone on a quiet corner with jazz, wine and a cigarette slowly burning in a fancy blue glass ashtray. The ashtrays no doubt are cleaned every two minutes and at least five break each time as they are so fragile. They are classy and pointlessly so, yet these small differences reassure the customer of the quality of his/her extortionate coffee! Which incidentally happens to cost more than ten of these ashtrays. I sound cynical, but I'm not, I laugh and find it all very endearing in perhaps an unfounded arrogant way. As I sit with my pen shaking in my hand I know that I have no reason to pity or belittle those who's comfort is so simple and harmless. The pen shakes as the alcohol reaches the nerves the blood and the need within me for comfort far harsher and more terrible than a useless blue glass ashtray. And the reality sets in! Oops meant to be meeting someone for drinks, obviously, because I would never make a date with anyone unless I was wanting sex or a drink, well that's almost true! I will on occasion be known to meet for coffee or a gallery visit but never the cinema as it is even lonelier than drinking alone.

I have never understood why its seen as such a romantic gesture to take someone to the cinema. No really, don't look at me like that, you know I am right. I suppose it's because you don't look at each other for ages, you don't say anything and you're surrounded by other people in the dark rattling popcorn; rustling sweetie wrappers and shushing each other in crescendo! At least that way there's no feet in mouths. (no that's not a reference to bovine toe nail issues).You can't ruin the date by saying the wrong thing until at least three hours in, which for many people (me included) means that the date has lasted through the 'shit date' time limit.

Its always the same,
But no-one can blame
The passion lashing our souls

Glad that you came,
It's only a shame
hiding and scared to unfold.
(you know you want to)

Please let me in
And let me begin
To release all the magic you hide

Give me a chance,
Not merely a glance
To be all that you hoped by my side
(you know you want to)

That pain that we share
Can be easy to bare
If combined we explode it as one!
Get rid of your dread,
Take me to bed
The time has come, dududuudgh♪♪

There are only a few days left in this busy city which I intend to waste spending money on useless items! Expensive coffees, free art galleries and solo cinema trips. It's surprisingly easy to spend 2 hours on a coffee especially at this price, and an hour walking to a gallery rather than spending £1 on a bus or running on a treadmill. Nothing very useful is achieved and yet your arms are full of bags your wallet is empty and you feel like you've run a marathon, and that's just by lunchtime.

Though there is much about London I dislike, there is nonetheless a lot to do, see and spend money on. Walking in the rain though, is free and one of the most enjoyable things London has to offer. There are far less people in the streets, there are always those who wait at the lights too close to the road and are surprised when a bus rushes past through a huge puddle and their Gucci suits get soaked! It makes me giggle and I have no qualms about turning and grinning about it to other bystanders. Unfortunately I do not like umbrellas, I like to feel the rain on my face, like the wind, it's a small reminder of nature in such unnatural surroundings. I say unfortunately, because women in London won't get their well groomed hair wet and many women are just the wrong height. If your hair isn't caught in the spokes; or you don't get trodden on because they can't see you; you can be damn sure you get poked in the eye! I actually believe that they are used as a weapon and defence shield all at once.

Still October

Fitting in is an essential for many Londoners and those who dare to say something to you at the bus stop or in a shop queue are either complaining, decades older than you or have a screw loose, maybe even two! I am one of these and yet I like to think that I have my screws well in place. A small gesture, smile or compliment is often met with a questioning look, and I love that. People are surprised and bewildered at unconditional kindness and seeing as I like to shock, and get a wee kick out of it, I do it as often as I can and not in any overt way.

You may well ask yourself, if she has time to write this how is she managing to talk to all these strangers, spend so much money and walk so much?" Which is precisely why I am about to lay this shaky pen to rest for a few hours while I venture back out into the streets and maybe spot something useful to do or even something not quite so useful, and maybe even waste a few more hours of the day.

Drifting through solitude
On world I know well
Where everyone is so damned rude
and impatient as hell.

Walking about with no soul,
Treading watery soil
Waking only to breathe
And watch the endless turmoil

Lost? Am I lost or found?
Found a path to lose myself in
Quiet, uncontaminated by sound.
Who knows what this pathway will bring
Perhaps a white rabbit hole underground.

Success! I have just wasted the grand total of 3 hours, swimming in a tiny pool surrounded by kids all in matching cossies being shouted at by red faced teachers amongst the splashes and giggles. Very refreshing, not entirely useless but clearly, I am ruining the effects by sitting in a pub with a customary glass of ruby liquid and the smoke of a smouldering Marlborough light in my eye. I feel I must add that it took me an hour to get here as I got myself completely lost, some how managing to get from Gloucester road back onto Gloucester road without doing three 90 degree turns in the same direction. In my mathematical opinion this is/should be impossible. Surely? Correct me if I'm wrong!!

Anyway I am now surrounded by a gaggle of pissed Russian woman taking copious photos of themselves, to remind themselves of how stupid they looked and why they took the photos before they went and got themselves totally leathered. Sorry really needed to say themselves loads of times just to de stress myself.

Oh a little anecdote, a friend once told me that if you want to invent a word for being drunk you add 'ed' to the end of any countable noun and put enough emphasis and feeling into the sentence and it works. Try it, I assure it does! Go on try!!! Eg.

"I got completely chair legged!" Or "God, he was totally ashtrayed." Maybe not the delicate blue glass kind in this case, but why not could be just a very classy drunk guy dressed in blue.

In case you haven't cottoned on yet I will be referring to drunken experiences throughout, so if you're sick of hearing stories that start "one time when I was really drunk I did this..." This was one if my dislikes of drinkers at university. The only thing anyone would talk about was "when I was out last night, pissed this happened," or "let's get drunk tonight nothing interesting happens unless we're pissed." Or the classic,

'I can't possibly dance unless I've had a few, I'll make a tit of myself', well that's for sure if you get twatted on the dance floor!!! In my opinion this is a sad reality for many students not interested enough in their studies. Wow, hold the phone! Literally.

Just got a random call from an ex boyfriend. I have not seen this man for two years. We had a very passionate affair in Paris while I studied there for the year. He has just phoned me out of the blue! Not entirely sure why, as he really didn't say much but it's nice to know the world is so small that he could have bumped into a friend of mine who had my number but also thought it would be a good idea to divulge my number without consulting me first. And actually while speaking to the ex the culprit was trying to get through, no doubt to warn me, a little late, but no harm done, and forgiven.

The problem with writing this is that I am not known for being discreet and in fact am very bad at keeping secrets especially secret about myself. I will have to sensor this and also promise to be imaginative enough to disguise characters in my life with some good effect. Although its good to tell the truth, so we are told, until it backfires in your face. I know that Gerald Durrel was inspire to write a second book, based on the fervent demand not to, by his family whom he describes in detail in the first.

Who the hell do you want me to be?
What the fuck do you want me to see?
Who the hell do you want me to be?
Let me be me, let me be free.
Life would be so good, if only I could
What if I should, and what if I could?
Please let me see me,
let the reflections free!
Reflect on me, and let it be.
Life was going to be so good,
If only I hadn't
If only I'd battled
Rattled
away into nothingness.

Another wet October day

Sometimes when the man of your nightmares turns out not to be bad enough to right him off as one of the lads or the same as the rest, you don't know what to do about it. How do you deal with someone who actually might care, you're sure he is wrong and that he is not really sure how he feel and yet he does everything right. Doesn't expect anything doesn't admit anything and let's you do what you want even though at the same time he says you are the only woman he will look at other than his mother, says you're beautiful even when spewing your guts out. Too good to be true Now unfortunately this guy is as romantic and sceptical as I am and possibly (if possible) has had as many bad experiences as I have. There is one thing I am sure he's right about. I should not tell him how he feels about me. (Though I know). In other words should I follow my ridiculous instincts as usual and get fucked over, role with it and then get him to leave me inadvertently by making him realise he's wrong without actually saying it or just enjoy it for once be positive 'till it goes tits up.(which it will)

I think I went off on a rambling tangent there. Might be a bit nervous of where this will go? Am I getting attached??Surely not. You can ask anyone thought, I really am that bad. As soon as anyone seems to like me for who I am and makes me feel I'm actually worth something, I run into bed with someone else. To make sure they are wrong. Really! It's true, and then I feel guilty, tell them and obviously expect to be sent packing! If you're inclined to do this to get rid of a boyfriend in a way that makes them feel like they are doing the breaking up, don't bother, it doesn't work. It's also plain wrong! Nine times out of ten you're forgiven(shite!!!). This is turning into a bit of a Bridget Jones which is not the purpose of this journal.

"What is the purpose?" I hear you cry, well none really, just want to log my thoughts before my memory is utterly drowned by alcohol abuse, and recounting what I do makes me realise how much I want to be somewhere else. It is also very good therapy. I have to take you on a journey with me to my home in the South of France, where I plan to start a self sufficient farm and vineyard, grow my own, veg, make my own jams and wine, get a cow for cheese and milk, and maybe meet a lovely farmer who will sweep me off my feet. Before I actually get there and begin this crazy venture(all on my lonesome) I feel I should let you into how I think and act in at totally different environment and in other situations ie here. There is nothing more different from a remote farmhouse in the Pyrenees than the bustle of London's high streets! Therefore you must bear with me until then, and anyway if you've followed so far, it's either because I've forced you to read this, or it's not as bad as all that, and you're enjoying my mindless ranting.

I love to watch,
The people that I see,
are not like me,
the things that they do,
are strange to me and you.
When things go wrong,
it's never for too long.
I love to watch.
The people around me seem free of pain,
the way they walk is plain, and yet insane.
In straight lines, fast and frantic.
In very straight lines full of panic.
Where is love where is passion?
I love to watch.
People in their treadmill give me despair
That life is so short, they just don't care
Where is the fear of death and waste

Has everyone like me lost their taste?
I love to watch,
From afar my chop sticks can't reach
my spoon is bent and the fork is melting.
A knife?

Middle of October, grey day

The last four weeks have been a whirl of new experiences both good and bad. I have embarked on a teaching course which I naively believed to be an easy task, it was not. After a holiday in the sun, getting up at five pm and doing nothing other than drinking and dancing; a nine to five where consciousness is a requirement, was much harder than anything I would inflict on my worst enemy. Nonetheless I stuck it out, and am now a qualified English teacher (only to foreigners) to those whose English is not fluent. Anyway the course was intense to say the least, 9-6 everyday with twenty minutes a day to yourself and then when you finally get home you have to plan the next days lesson 'till 1 am or three if your like me who drinks a bottle or two while studying. The worst thing is teaching with a panel of judges behind the class telling you how badly you've done. The best part of it is hearing your students telling you you're a great teacher even if technically you fail!! It's the only job I've done other than kindergarten where I feel I've made a difference and I wasn't even paid, I paid and it wasn't cheap. All in all I'm really pleased I did it and have another piece of paper on my pile of achievements. I hate the way people try to make you feel that you haven't wasted your time doing something, when you and they both know you have by saying the overly used phrase "You can put it on your CV!!" Complete pile of bollocks I'm afraid, people are more likely to notice what's on a public toilet door than on my CV. So if I ever hear anyone say it'll look good on you CV I'll rearrange their bloody CV. Sorry getting carried away again.

Sitting out of reach
On a branch of broken dreams
Singing sounds a screech
Nothing is as it seems

On the bus back to London

I've had a weekend out! Away from the trappings of London life let my hair down a bit and breathed less stuffy air for 24hrs. It felt great so forgive me if I rant even more than I have been. I've been all the way to the sunny shores of Oxford: sorry I lie, it pissed down the entire time, so much so that I actually bought a pair of shoes and socks from M&S because the bargain boots I purchased in Peter Jones the day before where bargain (non water proof) boots. Note to self:'Tabby if its cheap it doesn't mean it's a good deal!' Anyway the point is I went to Oxford saw a real friend and one that felt I should, you know the kind I mean. A friend who often calls for help, never offers anything and treats you badly most of the time and takes you for granted all of the time. Yet because they are so sad about their life or ashamed of their existence you feel you should make them feel better while they slowly drain your energy and joi de vivre without remorse. But then there are those you can not see or talk to for years and nothing has changed! The laughs the stories, smiles and tears are always as intense and fun! Those are the friends that make the others sufferable!

Lovely Sunday roast in a pub, rain through sunshine on the spires, beautiful architecture, and reminiscence of the good old days. All in all Oxford was beautiful and fun but peaceful too and a reminder of those special people.

OVERHEARD VOICES

Now back in London, Jazz, coffee and Marlborough lights. I have spent the morning wandering round the science museum and the

Natural history museum, not reading the educational bumph nor really taking in anything. I just zombied my way around scaring children with mindless facts, and staring blankly in front of me. Today due to Mr Not So Right ignoring me, I felt melancholy angry in a strangely passive way reminding me that I actually like him but not enough to mind that he said he'd call and didn't, and hasn't replied to my message. So clearly I've invited a friend over for karaoke and a piss up Saturday. In fact Mr Not So Right knows him and I have also been warned by him that if I do see this friend I will probably end up in bed with him. That is just outrageous!!!! My first reaction to this obviously was to immediately arrange to meet this friend (Saturday). Second reaction was to be insulted. Just because Mr Not So Right knows this friend better than I do and his reputation, shouldn't mean that I can't control myself!!? It is just plain rude. Though probably, knowing me and the fact that Mr N.S.R. has really pissed me off I might do it anyway out of spite (wrong I know) but I might enjoy it! Never let an opportunity slip by!

Anyway if that doesn't cheer me up I am meeting with a lovely man on Sunday, whom I met on my year in Paris 2yrs ago and fell head over heels for. (We were together briefly before he shot off back to America). I did at the time think I would see him soon after as he claimed to be looking for permanent work in Europe. Turned out to be a crock of shit and I clearly moved onto another but guess what! He has now found a permanent job, in London!! Just my luck, when I'm off to hermit myself in a life of seclusion and celibacy in Southern France.

I'm sure there's nothing more than friendship now anyway, yet I am excited to see him and hope I don't break down, say something stupid or do anything rash. I am quite capable of doing something I'll regret just to make him think "thank God I got out when I did, what a psycho!!" Not sure I really believe it's better to be remembered, even negatively, rather than not remembered at all.

This is all a few days away, it's only Monday! (Chill Tabby) Tomorrow I am off to Peterborough to see a friend of my Father's whom I have never met in my life. I am secretly hoping he will tell me a few secrets and paint a clearer picture of who my dad actually was, rather than the snippets of vague information I have had so far. Not knowing someone as a human but more as a myth, puts them immediately on a pedestal. Many people are too scared to tell me anything in case I break down, get shocked or they offend me. (I don't break down as often as I am making out) I am actually quite a level headed normal girl really. There is very little now that could shock me about my father, after finding two handmade moulds of his own penis while clearing out our old house. I have to say the craftsmanship was excellent, waxed rope and wooden door handles, but the 'thing' itself wasn't that impressive. He must have had quite an ego, and self confidence to get these made. The tattered old leather case containing these artefacts also contained other trinkets and lists, if anyone who knows me feels they want to know any more about this you can come and chat to me but seeing as this may land in some public metaphorical hand I feel it is only right not to say more. I do have morals after all!!

What am I doing? Where should I go?
Do I stop showing my feeling by now?
What is this feeling? Will it just grow?
I need to be certain of nothing somehow!
What is the meaning, how do I know?
When life has reached better than what is to come.
Where do I go then? Will I just know?
How does it feel now, will it all go?
Do I keep asking? Or shut the fuck up!
And go

I am surrounded today not by a gaggle of foreigners, though equally loud, but babies and toddlers. They are out in force and screaming their heads off. Generally speaking kids like me, I have funny hair, usually pink, weird clothes and an expressive face. Maybe I look a bit ridiculous or cartoon-like which means that they don't take me seriously. I don't have the first idea of how to look after them properly and would never inflict the world with one of my own, but for a few hours I love to play, teach and act like a fool. The innocence of a child shines through their eyes, have you noticed? Their eyes are huge and bright because they see the world, they actually take things in and even wonder why they look the way they do. Do you remember that feeling? Can you imagine really thinking anything is possible, something could be hidden behind a rock, everything is a new adventure. Nothing is taken for granted for kids, the chair I'm sitting on now turns into a den or climbing frame in seconds until, the child falls, cracks its head open, and screams blue murder. After that the chair becomes a chair again, not just any chair, an evil, ugly, nasty chair probably made by bad people who don't like sweets or children.

Right I can't take the yelling much more, my ear drums are aching; coffee is finished and I've somehow managed to chain smoke three cigarettes in the space of twenty minutes. This must be a sign, of what I don't know, but air, (though not fresh) is probably a good idea at this moment. Oh my God, now, not one but two, pregnant woman have walked in! Is someone up there trying to tell me something or is this babies and pregnant mother's day in Café Nero? I'm getting out of here before I catch immaculate conception!

Already missing the semi country of Oxford!!

We reproduce ourselves
We reproduce our mistakes
We learn from no-one
And give less than we take

We reproduce without care
We reproduce what is fake
Take take take this copy
Reproduce it again and again
Take take take my body
Withered and troubled by pain.

Haven't managed to get rid of this anger inside of me, in fact loads of insults are flying through my head. This is something I often do, plan what to say word for word, repeat it to myself so many times that I convince myself I actually said them. This way I haven't embarrassed myself, or chickened out, and feel a slight satisfaction that's utterly illusory (is that a word?) but almost could be real. I never actually phoned, and let this well rehearsed speech out. I'm going to have to visualise anger as a tangible creature that I can control and beat to a pulp!

Gonna hit this anger monkey so hard, just in my mind though. I have my boxing gloves on, and the rage in my step essential to flour an angry hallucination, with a left, a right, undercut!!!yes yes hahahah.

Ooh do I sound a bit too manic, I think so. Lets just pull its imaginary wings off instead. The fact that I've been walking for an hour dying for the loo and too stupid to just go into a restaurant and ask nicely hasn't helped my mood. I am now sensibly sitting in a weird bar full of eerie pictures of monsters and dead people, where the drinks are called Morticia and Frankenstein and other Halloween related names. My mood is now greatly improved especially due to the fact I have been to the toilet and have a glass of blood red wine resting on the coffin shaped table in front of me. The only thing they've managed to get really wrong in this pub is the music: the lights are low and mainly chandeliers; the menu says 'food to die for' and the whole atmosphere is killed by the jovial sound of ABBA playing in the background! Not really apt for a place called "The Black Widow."

Rainy October day

When I got home last night I made myself an enormous jug of sangria, which was lovely but gave me the not so clever idea of sending a text message to Mr N.S.R.. He had told me two days previous that he had been trying to forget me but in vain (how romantic) so my reaction yesterday after getting myself really raging was to tell him to forget me in the light hope that I would get an answer. I've often been told one of those annoying proverby type things, be careful what you wish for it may come true! It's a real shit when things other people tell you with that 'I told you so' grin on their faces comes true. There's no sign of a grin on my face, as after that I found it impossible to sleep and now hate myself for again having this ridiculous let down feeling when I actually asked for it. I'm sure I had convinced myself I couldn't get hurt if I didn't really care, but rejection even from a stray dog makes you wonder if you really do stink to high heaven.

I am on the train to Peterborough now, which reminds me of trips home when I was younger and visits to friends and yet this journey ends somewhere unknown. A destination where hopefully where an old man I've never met is going to recount stories of his antics with my father. I hope this will bring a smile to my face, I have a feeling from the stares of pity in the tube, that you can't avoid cause you're all sardines, that I look like a child who's blanket has gone for a wash! My comfort blanket has gone, and the smell will take days to return!

What really pisses me off is that I was determined not to fall in the trap again. I actually have no idea what's going on as this has been more of a phone relationship than a real one. The kind I like except for the no sex part, because there's no questions, no claustrophobia and no answers that have to be 100% true. One can be many things at a distance, it is easier to pretend to be something when no-one is there to witness it in person.

Fucking fuming now! Right have completely lost control of my anger and its wings have grown back twice the size. Tried to buy a ticket at the office where this po-faced woman sat asking me questions like "do you want the fast train or slow train?" I said "depends when they arrive"

"We'll ones quicker than the other" that's not what I asked you stupid bitch! She clearly thought I was mental but the fact is I had the departure time for the train I was being met at not the arrival, therefore there was a specific train I had to be on. When this was finally clarified they didn't accept my type of card. Seriously!!!!I mean I chose not to have a credit card because its not real money, if I spend money I don't have I will eventually have t pay it back. The fact that I have a card that only works if you really have money on it surely should make it a more reliable form of payment. Apparently not!!

"But the cash machines aren't working and the train leaves in less than ten minutes." (At eleven o'clock)

"I'm sorry but we don't control the cash machines or the type of cards we accept" and then one of those wee grins of satisfaction appeared and triggered the rage. I did find a cash machine that worked at 10:56 and got on the train but the tickets on the train obviously have to cost £20 more! Really!!! So I will attempt to calm with my tea and fag but the anger has grown a little more. I am now fuming and have just hung up twice on Mr N.S.R. Now beginning to regret it as I have no idea really if he has been ignoring me or not. He seems to have a plausible excuse, had he really lost his phone? Was I too rash to assume the worst? The point is that, if it effected me this much I like him too much and will inevitably get hurt so don't answer his calls and just get on with my journey alone!

I'm doing it again, going over what to say in my head, but if I don't answer the call I can't say anything stupid and I can also reach my own conclusions. Which are more than likely utterly unfounded and completely ridiculous, but there we have it, self denial or destruction is far more appealing than the dull facts aren't they. Ridiculous self made conclusions are always good especially when there is a risk of being proved wrong.

Well well well what a fantastic break from the city, green and copper foliage, trees and fields, real animals and fresh air! Cottage pie, proper conversations and blissful silence. I love the country and all the mud, blood and shit that goes with it.

A wonderfully reassuring, white haired chap I was met by at the station was full of enthusiasm, stories and advice. The comforting croaky voice of an elderly man, married with the slight stutter of someone trying to fit fifty years of stories into a two minute conversation (which actually lasted until ten thirty the following morning) were so familiar to me that I felt I had known this person forever.

What is strange about feeling a familiarity towards someone you have never met?
How do people meet anyway?
How do relationships begin, flourish and die?
Is there a part of yourself you are not aware of?
How much do we get told by our parents?
How much is inherent without needing nurture?
Are we a product of our parents genes or of their upbringing?
Who are we really?
Who am I really?
who

As we came into the pebble drive with a grand house peeking out behind the trees and the mist and rain surrounding it, I caught a glimpse of a stag in the field behind. Finally a glimpse of nature, a bit of life outside the concrete and a taster of what I will find in France. YIPEEEEEEE. This stag later turned out to be a very convincing sculpture which was in fact modelled on the type of stag found on Srathconnon (my Scottish roots). My father had lived in the highlands and done some stalking (not the creepy type) stags with this friend. The photos laid out on the coffee table were proof of their shooting trips in the beautiful heights of the Scottish mountains. All tweed and tartan, pipes and riffles and most of the posed pictures looked as if these men were contemplating the meaning of life or how to get back down in time for their wee dram!! Very inspiring photos with the most enthusiastic commentator on the sofa beside me! There was so much to tell, and the stutters did not stop my from drinking it all in with wonder. I couldn't have asked for a better nor more colourful account of my fathers past exploits. Stories ranged from shooting and fishing in the highlands; crazy gatherings and drunken nights, to working in the Savoy hotel, escorting beautiful film stars from the airport back to the hotel.

There were wonderful smells from the kitchen where the loveliest lady had been slaving over an Aga while I and her husband talked and talked and talked, no time for air or pause. She is one of these natural mothers: looks comfy like a teddy bear; smells of baking; full of hugs and smiles. She cooked away furiously singing away while we chatted. There was far too much to be said, far too many questions to be asked and such a restriction on time, that we both at times sounded like race commentators.

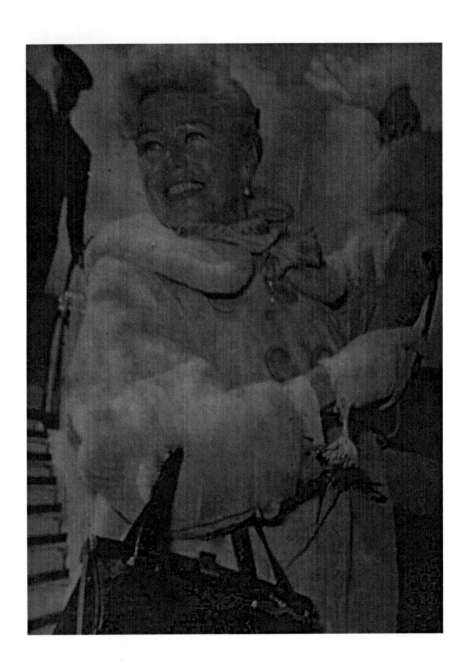

Dinner came as a great relief and both our mouths were pleased of an excuse for rest. The steaming hot cottage pie was devoured gratefully. Their hospitality amazed me as I had never really met them before, or maybe so long ago I couldn't remember and yet I was treated beautifully, with flowers in my room, a glass of wine with my bath which I always find indulgent even when I'm alone at home! I had had a wonderfully reviving stay, and a great reminder of the true value of friendship and kindness, not to mention the peace and rejuvenation the country offers. I am going to miss those copper leaves going red and brown at the edges. I love the way they look like they are burning and on fire as you watch them even in the pouring rain. These autumn colours remind me of bonfires, fireworks, Halloween parties and half-terms. So many memories are flying back to me now, and so many new ones I never knew existed, all swirling in Scottish mistiness.

♪*Come by the Hills, by The Corries*♪
Oh come by the hills,
Te the land where fancy is free
Stand where the peat meets the sky
And the lochs meet the sea

....

Oh come by the hills
to the land where life is a song
And the cares of tomorrow can wait until this day is done.

I will soon be up in Scotland for my brothers and best friend's birthdays, which both happen to be on Halloween itself. Unfortunately Aberdeen is itself dark, grey, noisy and ultimately a city but all this is forgotten when I know I am going to see the greatest and amazingly awesome creature ever created. If there were such a thing as the perfect human being, fascinating, talented, funny, interesting and yet full of lovely faults that you can't help forgiving, this would be the best example of such a creature. Someone like this must be treasured and respected and although I do know how lucky I am to know her I fail her in those respects a little too often, but the feeling is mutual.

23

Still October

I have now arrived back in London Kings Cross creating a dull thud to my wondering imagination. For a few moments as the train chugged slowly along, I was in the depths of the mountains in France, planting seeds, cutting wood and being happy. The mountains where I will be beginning my future and making my dream home. But reality awaits now and France is a few weeks away. And in the meantime although London and Aberdeen are not the hills and mountains of the highlands or Pyrenees there is plenty of mischief to be achieved! And I intend to achieve it, with or without help, starting today with a visit from Mr N.S.R.'s mates from Spain who has moved to Brighton. He can't make Saturday after all and is turning up this afternoon. I am heading back to the flat to put some war paint on my face and perfume all over. The reputation preceding this man need a shield.

Things are not always what they seem!!!

Well what a surprise, lovely down to earth guy with glasses and no particular presence, arrived at Victoria station at five on the dot. We went for a Starbucks mocha which was a novelty for him, the coffee culture hasn't hit Spain yet and working in a restaurant in Brighton wouldn't give him any reason to have long coffee breaks in all the chain coffee shops, as I seem to be doing at the moment.

Anyway the longest coffee ever was had, it went dark and we moved outside to smoke so clearly at that moment it pissed down with rain! Typical! What to do now? Well this friend had been told that I sculpted and painted but the only way to see them would be at an Internet café which just seemed a stupid thing to come to London for. I used this moment as a great excuse to take a foreigner to see a show, and secretly really wanted to go to a musical myself!!!So clearly we ended up watching Chicago on the strand after quickly washing down a pizza with a bottle of Rioja.

It was fabulous, I mean really fabulous!!!!!I was instantly reminded of all the reasons why I had wanted to join the theatre so many times, why I have always loved singing dressing up and putting on a show. He had never been to a musical before let alone one of the biggest shows currently in London theatres. It was great, we laughed clapped whistled (sometimes at the wrong times) and as I translated more complicated bits, I also tried to sing along. He told me that the best part wasn't the play itself but the enthusiasm and joy with which I was explaining it.

It is a very sexy and deeply erotic performance and I do have a soft spot for dancers bottoms! All that jazz was much appreciated by both parties and as we left the theatre with the knowledge that his train left in half an hour, we came to the silent conclusion that it would be missed accidentally on purpose. We ventured out into the pouring rain, singing and dancing with an umbrella used more as a prop than shelter. Suddenly we were in a musical, dancing through London. We danced our way along the strand and into a dingy club in Leicester square, passers by sniggering but not laughing outright when I manage to flip the umbrella inside out while doing one of my amazing dance moves. Well they are amazing to me in my head anyway. The reason I say not laughing outright is because it's not the British thing to do. The weather, the rules, the people and the sentiment is always a little half hearted, the British don't do extremes in general. Of course there are the wonderful exceptions to the rule!!!!

We arrived quite early in this club and it was therefore empty, luckily this man is just as much of an exhibitionist as I am and also was just as drunk. We had the dance floors to ourselves and used every inch of them as dramatically as possible. Our antics continued for what seemed an age until the place filled out and eventually became crammed with people, not really dancing (half heartedly, not to repeat myself but none the less true).

Lovely evening all in all and we took a taxi home where I left and sent my guest onwards to Victoria to catch some nocturnal train home, not realising that in fact he ended up in Gatwick airport where he fell asleep missed his connecting train and didn't get home till 7am. (oops) Now, I could have invited him in, but as I knew that inevitably we would end up in bed together as I really have no will power, regardless of what I might say, I was very pleased with myself for finding a plausible excuse by saying it wasn't possible.

You were the one,
But time did come,
When you and I fled love, shed love.
Like a second snake skin love.

Look into my eyes from underneath
Can you see what I see just out of reach?
You were the one but time did come

Don't you even try to teach!
I'm teaching myself to be a bitch

Look into my eyes from just bellow
can you feel and attempt to grow?
You were the one, but time did come.

Don't you ever think you know
I am telling myself to go

Look again and look at me
look at what you'll never see
Be the fool they say not to be,
Do that which they tell you to flee
I want to be free
You were the one but time did come
I want to be me
Let me be

Clearly seeing as we are reliving one of my nights out, something had to go wrong! I had carefully put my bag and coat in the nightclub's cloakroom, because I always loose things. I was already on phone number 8 in less than a year and didn't want to risk loosing this one too. I am about to be on phone number nine. Yes the bag I had the phone in was zipped shut, and I don't remember taking it out before handing the bag in. The pocket with the phone in it was still sipped shut on its return to me. However when I got home at four there was no longer a phone in it! What did I do between leaving the club and getting home? I got in a taxi, could I remember what cab, no.! Just my luck and I was drunk so decided to phone all the numbers I could think of from the land line, in order to get Brighton man's number. I had a pathetic and unfounded hope that I may have given it to him for safe keeping. I had no recollection of ever doing this but fingers crossed! No, obviously no! But I did find out he had missed his connection, and was waiting for the next train in two hours time.

Having woken my sister at five in the morning and then Mr N.S.R. who both understandably were not too pleased of a drunken early morning call and told me where to go in not such polite words. I decided it was a useless venture and settled with the thought or knowledge that I would be phone less for a few days before a replacement came from the phone company. Yes yes, I have learned my lesson, I am insured for a lost or stolen phone now and don't have to fork out for a new one each time I have a night out. I would think that the phone company would raise my monthly bills to make up for this.

There is something strangely fine about not being able to be contacted and in my case, having no identity as every piece of ID I do have, has also recently been stolen. It's great and means I can be what I want, go anywhere without too many calls or questions but it does mean I can't leave the country, this will prove to be a problem when I try to catch a flight in two weeks time.

I feel like a complete chicken and feel I should say that some inappropriate kissing and Chicago like dancing did take place last night in the club, which is why I felt so good about myself for not inviting 'said kisser' home. There was a short drunken discussion on whether this was inappropriate behaviour or just a normal part of a fun evening, the natural course of which involves kissing whomever you are with as a general rule (we made that up on the train). The result of this is that my conscience is not tarnished my ego slightly boosted and my sex life potentially enhanced and increased by one candidate. What a great time we live in!

This evening I am meeting an old friend of my mother's, who in fact is a friend of mine too. He reminds me of, a slightly less made up and elaborate version of, boy George. He is camp, fun and quite knowledgeable about theatre, people to know and great on gossip. We are Sohoing tonight, Well I hope so!!!but let's see!

FUN FUN FUN!!!!

Yeeha

Such a different world at night, and in certain streets and areas of London. One minute you are surrounded by suits and ties, then the next its drag queens, and cocktails!

Less rainy October day

I Did go to the passport office today to check how things were getting on after I reported the stolen item, but then realised that I really am a dunce at times! I filled in the police report but no passport application, so I haven't in theory even applied for a new one! **Stupid**. This obviously means I will miss my flight which is after all only in two weeks and I know there is no way I will get a new passport before then! AGH!! My plans of heading to Aberdeen on Monday are shot to hell too because I have to wait three working days for my phone, obviously I couldn't have lost it on Monday, no Thursday! With the weekend in the middle three working days takes us to Monday at least. Which means it'll come Tuesday if I'm lucky, almost an entire week later! I know shut up!!!first world problems! I surprisingly insured it, so will get a replacement without having to fork out any pennies. When oh when will a passport come though?!

Clearly all my plans have turned to shit as I have no phone and no means of contact and no identity! But that means I am free to do what ever I want and be whomever I want to be. I'm sure yesterday I felt the opposite, but totally forgotten now! I am now in a Chinese restaurant, surrounded by Chinese people awaiting a film at the cinema just down the road, yes alone. Oh well never mind a quiet night will no doubt do me some good and yes, I am not so keen on Chinese food, but its so much easier to waste time when you have to eat with two tiny sticks.

Another wee anecdote here. My favourite speech, that we had at school assembly religiously once a year, was about chopsticks.

A man dies and is at the gates of heaven but before entering he is taken to hell, to see what he has been saved from. Hell is a huge banquet hall, full of people and piled high with wonderful looking food an impressive feast. 'Why is that so bad?' I hear you ask. Well everyone there is withered hungry angry and starving despite all the food. The only way they can eat is with 1 meter long chopsticks,(and I was complaining about my 4inch ones). The man leaves perplexed and enters the gates to heaven. The same scene awaits him there! Any yet everyone in heaven is happy and well fed. They also have to eat with 1 meter long chopsticks and yet they do not starve. The man asks what the difference is, the answer comes in a very matter of fact way. The people in hell are selfish and evil and only try to feed their own appetites, those in heaven are generous and share the food. They feed each other with their chopsticks. This lesson can be used in life generally. If life is hell and going badly one should look not to the outside effects but what we may be doing to cause this discomfort ourselves.

How the hell do you eat Chinese without looking uncouth! I mean I am managing to get it all over myself, you can't cut anything because there is no knife!!!! They have these huge veg things that are too big to fit in in one bite but also too slippery to hold and bite. What to do? Oh the trials of life!(Stop complaining)

The shittest part is that I seem to be mechanically piling on the pounds as if subconsciously I believe I will starve if I live in a remote house in the mountains! Trying to grow my own food with the nearest restaurant, be it Chinese or any other, one hours drive away. Actually I think they have a kebab place in my local town! They recently discovered the Internet, so there is now actually one cyber café but only kids and me seam to use it. There is still no internet at the house, and the phone is at the end of a very long line so regularly gets cut in a storm. The local kids go to the Cyber Café for games and me well, for everything except games. No-one with email business would be seen dead there I'm sure!

DREAMS
Dreams because they are not real
dreams because they are what I feel
dreams can come true
not for you not for you!!

Because I have imagination
Because I love temptation
Dreams will never come
Dreams are all gone

Today my dreams came true
Today I am losing you
I am finding someone else
I dream of somewhere else
I'm speaking of myself!

Wake up in the sun,
froliking and fun
vapours
DREAMS

I really can't wait to be out there. I'm building this up so much that when I finally do get there and my work begins it will only be a massive let down to you and me, or maybe not let's be optimistic not realistic! Best way to be!

Right off to the movies now that I have successfully gotten most of this black bean sauce decoratively all over the table the book and me.

Am sitting at home now in silky trousers with a cup of tea and feeling extremely relaxed after a good film. It has been ages since I saw Mr N.S.R., and if we are meant to be having some kind of relationship it may be an idea to communicate a little more. Think I'll give Mr N.S.R. a call as I am in a good mood and can't possibly argue about anything. When I'm alone, conscious and tea is involved I feel warm and cuddly, this sounds ridiculous but its just the type of times romantic conversations, hand holding and hugging should be done. The day after a weekend bender for instance, you just want tea hugs and a romcom! Or is that just me?? With these thoughts in mind I dial the dreaded number. Clearly 'Foot-in-mouth' is my middle name, everything comes out wrong resulting in Mr N.S.R. hanging up after saying some cryptic

Spanish proverb completely incomprehensible to me. Yet another night without sleep and with mixed phrases and emotions swimming around my head. What happened to the sweet hand holding type evening, romantic conversations and just being comfy? It all went to shit, that's where it went! Telling each other we really miss each other, and can't wait to be together again, shame. Maybe it's just not the truth. What the hell is wrong with us? and what the hell did he say before he hung up? All I can remember is that it was something to do with peaches and shade? Have no idea what it meant but I'm sure it wasn't "you are a lovely peach who should get out of the shade," more like "peaches rot in the shade like you!" I'm ranting again sorry. What about "you are a shady rotten peach"? Oh shut up Tabby.

Give me peace
Give me the flowing of silky skin,
Give me the touch of velvet eyes
Give me the heart you store within
Give me peace like the endless skies

Give me your time and think on me
Give me your arms surrendering strength
Give me wake with cups of warm tea
Give me shelter and song at length

Give me days of games and glory
Give me weeks of shameful blissful
Give me dancing dashing stories
Give me life with every kiss

Give me all you can and more
Give too much while asking naught
Give me promise of what's in store
Give me a break,
As if!

Yet another wet day in October

Anyway I have been wondering round today half conscious again, feeling low, talking to myself and found a great way to spend another limbo day. I went to see the dinosaurs in the natural history museum. Beautiful building full of wonders. Children smiling, running, wowing and whirling around me, always cheers me up. At one point I was in the sea life area, where two young girls were looking at a picture of a squid apparently eating a whale. I in my all knowing friendly way butted in with "we'll no, actually the whale is getting cleaned see, the squid eats all the bugs of it its great, like a squid shower." You can imagine the looks of horror on their faces. "Mummy mummy a scary pink haired girl spoke to us! She was really scary mummy!" I wasn't surprised at their reaction but it did shut me up and stopped me grinning and pulling faces at any of the other kids around, in case I got dragged away by security.

Have resorted to a safer pastime, drinking solo in a small secluded pub, and to be even further from anyone have ventured to the empty beer garden with the threat of rain upon me. Guaranteed solitude. It's actually quite nice, the trees are rustling in the wind there is no sound of cars and I can't even hear the bustle from inside the pub, could almost not be in London.(Big grin on my face!!!!helped by the wine I'm sure, but at least no-one is here to look at me, and assume I escaped from the nearest asylum).

The great thing about mobiles is that you can text and not get your words mixed up or put your foot in it. Deleting texts over and over before eventually deciding it is risk free enough to be sending it is a classic, who has not done it?? Apologised to Mr N.S.R. and was not only forgiven but asked to forgive his equally abrupt reaction. I was also asked to be patient which is not my forte, I haven't seen him for months now so I don't suppose another will make much difference. But seriously! I don't think anyone takes kindly to being told to BE PATIENT!!! Seeing as I have no passport or identity I'm not likely to be leaving the country any time soon. I would usually be craving sex and jumping on anyone willing but I'm not feeling very attractive or sure of myself at the moment. Mr N.S.R. doesn't help with that much, he is far away, not particularly romantic or demonstrative. The fact I am in limbo: waiting to move; wondering aimlessly around London; and putting on weight while spending money on pointlessness is making my spiral into self doubt all the more immediate. I am however having more and more erotic dreams which is clearly my subconscious feeding the craving. 'What on earth is wrong with that?' I hear you shout!!! The problem is that I went off masturbation years ago, it just gets boring now, well the thought of it really, as it's been years, so I can't even pass the time that way! I had a slight accident when I was younger and discovered masturbation. When you discover something great it is difficult to get enough of it, and well, like many youngsters I went too far! Possibly a little addicted, and with all addictions there is eventually an overdose, resulting in a hospital or prison. Put me off for life!

Now sitting in the same swish bar with blue glass ashtrays with Art, the man I met in Paris two years ago. He has run off to the toilet so will be brief, too late oops he's back will resume later.

We had lunch in a Spanish Tapas bar, giving me a chance to show off my language skills. He had attempted to impress when we were in Paris, by taking me to a crèperie which coincidently had Bodelaire poetry books right next to our table.(No coincidence at all!) He began to read a romantic poem to me, and then the waitress came for our order. Oh dear, he realised I was fluent in French and may not have been as impressed with his French as he had hoped. I had an inner giggle as he cringed, but far too polite to say he had made a bit of a tit of himself trying to show off to me. In the tapas bar, I was surprisingly allowed to order which was a reminder of the very first time we met for lunch. He had ordered for me, which he thought was very romantic and thoughtful but really pissed me off! I am a bit fussy but also aware that I can be a control freak. How dare he assume to know me so well on our first meal out? I am so much more mysterious than that, or I like to think that I am. Anyway after about two hours we were the only people still in the restaurant and thought that maybe they actually close for lunch or something. We walked and talked about where he should live, reminiscing about my hovel in Paris where I froze almost to death. He has given me a lovely fur lined coat that year as a Christmas present, precisely because he was so worried about me dying of cold, and also gave me the music for 'La Bomème', hahhaha. I did live in a very bohemian flat, with a very narrow windy staircase that never had light. The amount of times I came in after a bar crawl with my flat mate, and nearly killed myself on those stairs!! The sockets in the walls were falling out, the wires hanging out. I decided to stick them back to the wall with thick tape as security. We also had two electric hobs, that worked occasionally, and if both were used at the same time and got a little wet the electricity would cut out in the entire flat. I never knew if there would be water, if there was, would it be hot? The 'bed room' was the attic, with a very low ceiling. It took me months not to systematically bang my head on the ceiling every morning. It's not the nicest way to wake up, in fact almost guaranteed you wake up raging. I adored that flat, and he would worry every time he visited.

After the walking and talking we then stopped in a bar where the conversation became inevitably a little more relaxed but serious if you see what I mean. The subject being more serious and the inhibitions having been drowned a little.

Had I met a potential life partner or ever thought about it? This question got a short yes and a meaningful look that shut him up instantly and moved the conversation onto children. You can imagine by the time I got home I was in such a muddle I rang Mr N.S.R. immediately and ranted incomprehensibly at him. There are clearly questions one does not ask! It was pointless but I ended up asking his advice, clearly wanting some meaningful promises of some sort. The promises never came. I sat on the sofa contemplating where I was going, what I wanted from life, and who! If he was unwilling to be with me what was I waiting for? Why was I kidding myself? I sat moping, depressed but….. Mr N.S.R had made no promise but surprisingly he was concerned enough to phone again, yippee. My mood was immediately lightened and my morale no longer scraping the floor. He let slip that he did care lot about me but hadn't thought of the future. Utter bull if you ask me, he was just worried about me going off with someone else. Maybe he just had no other options available to him at the time, he is quite a flirt,(pot kettle black). I do know he is unsure, and not necessarily head over heals about me, but was nice to hear never the less.

Contradictions and confusions
confuse and corrupt
care cuddle and caress me
your doubt will be stopped

All doubting and deceitfulness
denied all my life
do deeds that destruct me
result in your strife

re evaluating my thoughts
reliving as two
refusing my fears
realising you
we are now a wonderful one
where, why, when?
No answers will come
My wish has come true now,
My wish is you now!
Or is it,,,,,,

So with all these crazy mixed thoughts I got myself on the Megabus to Aberdeen which left at midnight, with a bag full of goodies for the two Halloween birthdays.

What a strange bus journey. I mean really what the hell is this? Got a call from Mr N.S.R. who wanted to check I had calmed down. (cheeky bastard!) While phoning a strange computerised music came on almost like a mobile phone ring tone. It got increasingly louder so I turned to the Oriental girl behind me accusingly, meaning she turn what ever obnoxious music she was listening to down!. She looked just as bewildered as I did, and I realised she was not the culprit. The music then stopped for two seconds and another equally obnoxious sound started and at this point Mr N.S.R. began doubting I really was on a bus. The entire coach was in fits, and the driver was almost bent double with laughter as he came up the stairs to the second flour to do the passenger count.

A huge, confident and smiley black driver greeted us with a strong London accent "int dis grea! Megabus what a reck, nextime ill be play station, bar, DVD's vhe lot." By this time I had lost track of Mr N.S.R.'s conversation and was in fits of giggles myself. Cramped into a tiny space next to an eight year old, unhappily winging about not to have his brother's seat next to mum, the thought of a bar and DVD's was hilariously unimaginable. Awful seats and a twelve hour journey how could the conductor actually have made it sound like a playground ride (which I love). It was a great way to introduce his passengers to the ride of their life.

Inverness, not Aberdeen

Anyway, arrived in Inverness rather than Aberdeen because I had missed the change over of buses, but wanted to see my cousin anyway, who was visiting her dad in Scotland for the first time in two years. She lives in Spain with most of the rest of my family. I thought it would be nice to see her out of her usual working environment, ie a dodgy bar full of drunks and old gamblers.

It was freezing!! We met in town, shopped, drank coffee and went to the cinema. It was short but great fun, a good old catch up. Relaxed no stress just what the doctor ordered. We talked about family, her work and love lives (mainly mine). The bar she works in is the regular watering whole for Mr.N.S.R, so she knows him fairly well, and has eyes and ears in places I can't. It is a little embarrassing as she witnessed me run off to bonk someone for an hour while Mr N.S.R. sat at the bar with his father, I had just met for the first time the day before. I was at the bar having coffee explaining what I had the intention of doing, she was confused understandably, and I went off while Mr.N.S.R was still sleeping in the flat. When I returned he was having coffee in the bar with my cousin having full knowledge of what had just happened. Oops.

It has in the past been a terrible habit of mine, to jump into bed with someone else when things are getting too serious. In this case the 'other guy' was a very young, very camp, very pretty gay boy with a little diamond piercing on his upper lip, and not a hair on his body. Terrible mistake! Needless to say my cousin knows me well and doesn't judge me, she just listens and agrees when I tell her how much of a tit I am. Easy to agree with.

The next day I went to Aberdeen and arrived while best friend was in choir practice with a dodgy phone (as usual). There was no way to get in touch with her, and there was no way of knowing where to meet her. So phoned my bro and went over to sit at his flat until Shmona could come and pick me up (will call her Shmona as she smokes a lot).

The greatest shock was for her to see me sober at my brother's flat (a rare occurrence). I had cut down over the last two days and was already experiencing withdrawal symptoms (sweating at night and belly ache during the day). Still, the point was I was going to party this weekend without embarrassing any of my friends or family. This meant pacing myself on the alcohol front. The general haze was subsiding, and the result was not a pretty sight, but all in all very good for me and those around me.

I was very happy to see that Shmona, she had a good group of friends beside her, around her and in lectures. She usually has downs, confidence problems and incredible self doubt which I saw was being banished by these people and her work. A wonderful thing to witness, someone you care about clearly in the right place and the right people.

Met Shmona in a pub after choir where her and the other singers hang out, this was brilliant as I realised that although a strange group of all shapes and sizes they really have a good laugh and obviously sing alongs.

Had an early night and went shopping for Halloween decor the next day! Needless to say we got very carried away had a late lunch and returned with only a couple of hours to spare before guests arrived. PANIC!! In this time, Shmona and I dressed up and decorated frantically. While she calmed her nerves with vodka I tidied and tried to keep her calm. When eight o'clock came, no guests arrived so obviously she got miserable and thought not a soul would turn up. She was clearly wrong. Not only was the small lounge heaving with witches, devils, ghouls and even a sailor but a piper came and played the pipes.

The bag pipes is a sound many people don't love like I do. My cousin says it reminds her of funerals (true for me too), but, that means it reminds me of family too which is a nostalgic moment. I felt I had to share it. I Phoned Mr N.S.R. as I know he had never heard it before, the reaction was understandable "all I can hear is a horrible drone and loads of people" "that's it yep isn't it great!" My enthusiasm was not exactly shared but none the less he got a sample of pipes from Scotland!

The evening ran smoothly with cake, singing and the dreaded "cereal box game." I clearly initiated this as I absolutely love it and know that it breaks the ice, keeps people entertained and costs nothing.

Shmona was first to bend down and attempt to pick up the box with her mouth without touching the ground with anything but her feet. While her purple horns flashed in the dark the crowd chanted "go Shmona go Shmona bend it like its your birthday." Ironically she was bending over and it was her birthday!!!I know nothing compared to discovering Penicillin, but still! It was brilliant, but unfortunately for me, I had to do this with my bum aimed at the TV as I was wearing the tiniest skirt (belt really) suspenders and see-through ish hot pants. I had also put on a purple glow in the dark tinkerbell wig and painted my face like a slightly dead almost skeletal woman. Not a pretty sight, but hey its Halloween.

(Would just like to say that while I write this I have just sat in a London bar and ordered a red wine which cost me more that five pounds! For a glass!)

I woke up sore, bewildered and on the floor the next day with some random on my left and another sprawled on the floor amongst the party poppers (popped), crisps and general debris. Also I had a slight hang over for the first time in years because I had paced myself and not been excessive for about four days now. The body was wondering what I was up to!!

Needless to say Saturday started late, like 13oclock in the morning late and I again spent a lazy day at my brothers watching films, till the evening where Shmona and I were preparing for Salsa. This was surprising to me who knew Shmona not to be a dancer, and had been told just how evil I had been dragging her to clubs persuaded she really did like it. I was convinced that someone with so much energy had to like dancing, and as much as me, so for a year when we lived together in London, I would insist on taking her to clubs with the certainty she was having a whale of a time, when actually secretly she was hating every minute of it! So as we sat in her room on the small single bed, dressing and making-up while a bottle of red slowly but surely evaporated.

Turns out no-one wanted to come with us and we decided instead to go to karaoke. I may have been persuaded by her, and now realise she was probably relieved and grateful as hell to all her friends for flaking. The taxi we flagged down gave us the ride for free seeing as Shmona was on such a high, had a toy monkey with her and didn't stop talking and giggling and smoking. He was instantly under her charm, and laughed the whole way.

The place was a dive full of middle aged red faced alcoholics, some with their young kids and some trying not to fall over as they swayed to the horrific band playing. The band consisted of four elderly men. The one on the guitar who kept reminding us that today was charity day. They needed it! The singer was spindly, like a rag doll that's lost it's stuffing. He wore cringe worthily tight cream jeans and banged a tambourine against his thigh through every song that he attempted to sing.

The vodka and coke came in a tiny dirty glass with no ice and hardly any actual drink either, I couldn't actually bear to even put my lips to the glass and infect myself by drinking the glass of wine I ordered! Before long I suggested we leave and we dashed out into the streets in fits of giggles and strolled into a half Indian bar half nightclub.

The upstairs had Indian rugs and pillows on the floors in small alcoves with low tables. Downstairs was the dance floor, darkly lit, with a very high stage where the DJ's played. The two DJ's were dressed as a cardinal and a priest, Shmona and I were the only people there to begin with. The dance floor was incredible. Shmona came to check it out with me reluctantly, I knew she would rather chill out on the cushions and drink. It was wooden but with springs under it, like a sports court, so that even if you didn't want to dance you have to, more so if its heaving with other dancers.

As I write

(Am waiting for my passport and am drinking a glass of wine while smoking awful fags. A blond, scruffy young looking Fin has just come to sit with me. He was hovering near my table, looking for a place to sit no doubt, He seems harmless enough, with his rucksack and 'look at me I'm travelling' clothes on. He says he is waiting for a friend unconvincingly. I do realise he's lying when he says he's waiting for a friend, especially when I hear the rest of what he has to say. I don't offer a bed for the night, when he unsubtly let's slip he has nowhere to stay especially as it is not my flat and he could be a psycho, or a pervert. He doesn't seem like one, to be honest he is just a kid looking for a free place to stay the night. I have offered him a seat at my table, but a bed is too much. I definitely do not offer anything more when he tells me he's good at four things; Speaking English, throwing a ball, flying a plane and eating pussy! Really???? Are you fucking kidding me!!!!! Needless to say I finished my glass sharpish and got the hell out of that pub! But I did promise to email, so I won't. How the hell do I attract these freaks? I mean seriously, he didn't look that desperate for a place to stay, but maybe he was. Anyway who the hell says that kind of thing! Really! In all honesty if he had been better looking I would have finished my glass slower, maybe even gotten another and one for him. Shame for him he wasn't.)

Stop don't go therefore
Stop stop why do you care
Shut the whole that says that shit
I'm alone cause I fucking love it!

Stop that wasn't me
Stop I'm so sorry
Couldn't stop the truth coming out
All I want to do it shout

Stop right there right now
Stop telling me how
Need your balls and not your brain
And to you it's all the same

Stop that wasn't me
Stop I'm so sorry
I need to feel, and feel to breathe
What you have is just beneath

Breath it all without the blame,
Beneath your balls beneath your brain
You don't get a thing I feel.
What you have to do is kneel

Stop that was me, stop I'm not sorry
Take your balls and you're brain
Never come near me again!

Anyway back to the weekend in Aberdeen.

Sunday was Halloween and therefore my brother's actual birthday. He was expecting me at his place at some point in the day, obviously I was in the pub with Shmona till about 5pm but none the less got to his to give him his pressies, lovingly but not very carefully picked out, and help decorate with spider's webs and pumpkins. I love decorating which is good as there is a lot to be done to the house when I move to France. Shmona had been slightly humiliated by me over the last few days, only because I wanted her new friends to have some funny stories of her past to recount. Maybe also to show them that we have a strong bond! When I lived with her in London we also lived with a guy whom I did not like at all and found creepy and lecherous. One evening however I walked past the bathroom and heard Shmona shouting out "you're so sexy, you're so sexy, you're so sexy." Clearly my mind went wild! My initial thought was shock and "Shmona what the fuck are you doing he's a creep!" The door was slightly ajar, so…..Yes I did, I really did, I know I shouldn't have but I did. I stupidly peaked through, only to find Shmona in front of the mirror shouting at her reflection with great enthusiasm. "You're so sexy you're so sexy." With fists clenched and determination in both faces.

This story I told over a post choir dinner, the other food for gossip was the birthday present I decided on giving her when enough friends were present but not so pissed that they would forget. She had originally asked me for mascara so clearly I got a wee make up kit but the best part of the gift was a bright pink vibrator with a pink fluffy case which had the words 'wild bitch' printed on the side. She didn't admit to me until the next day that she was actually very pleased with the gift as the embarrassment and shock got the better of her. I do adore her, and have forgiven her so much, and she me. I was surprised she got so upset about this gift. In a way it was just to show her new friends how close we were and that she was a fun girl. There was a moment is our past that made me assume that these things were ok. My first ever sexual encounter, not concentual but none the less with a boy I thought I loved, was worsened by the fact that the very next day after taking my virginity, when I was neither ready nor old enough, he decided to begin flirting outrageously with Shmona. She did not refuse his advances, as she had no idea what had happened and after having been humiliated physically I was to endure a mental and emotional torture of seeing them swooning all over each other. I decided it was better to forget forgive and move on for everyone's sake. So I thought the gifts would be taken lightly,. She admitted it was more the company that was uptight, and might be shocked and not her. We never know other people's minds and reactions though do we.

I did not give my brother any such embarrassing or interesting present, seeing as he generally forgets mine or makes little if no effort

I didn't feel that I had to go into much detail when choosing a gift. I adore him though, so wanted at least to give him a token gift and card to show I care. His party was quieter and smaller than Shmona's, mostly due to the size of the flat and the presence of a seven year old child. The cereal box was none- the less brought out again, and I seem to remember charades, absolutely adore that game. There is a funny telepathic thing between my brother and I that means if he does a cryptic circle with his finger, much to everyone's confusion, I know he means a chameleon! It infuriates most other players, and very quickly we are not allowed to play that game on the same team, or generally together at all. It's not technically cheating though is it!!? The game didn't last ages as everyone go bored of us winning. A strange guy called Cosmo appeared at some point, dressed as Satan, in the evening and I painted the faces of a few guests who had made no effort to dress up. All in all a fairly normal Halloween party!

My brother and friends had a great time and Shmona turned up which was a great relief to me as I was beginning to talk a load of shit to a very cute friend of my brother's. It is a common reaction to stressful situations but luckily I was rescued in time by my loyal friend. This friend of my brother's was dressed as The Phantom of the Opera but looks more like a Smirf in reality. Smirf and I have ended up in bed on several occasions, most of which I was too embarrassed to recall, and have since apologised for. At the point in the proceedings that Shmona arrived I was rudely insinuating that he had a small penis in front of all his friends. (another defence mechanism, to imply that I am not interested).It was a joke and luckily taken as one. Yet again we ended up in bed together. I woke with a familiar "oh god I'm naked, what?..." But this time I remembered most of it, didn't pass out on the poor boy and he hadn't actually gone by the time I was fully awake!

Clearly I haven't seen or heard form him since but this is generally what happens and better that it stays that way. I have no intentions of telling Mr N.S.R. for that matter unless the topic should come up. A lie can only be a lie if said. If nothing is said nothing is said, the best tautology ever! Really Tabby ya think! I know this is a shit excuse and has been used a lot in the wrong circumstances but I have made no promises to anyone (in those terms) and therefore feel I have done nothing wrong. It's beginning to sound like I'm trying to convince myself that I have done nothing wrong!No need I haven't, so I'll stop now before I start feeling guilty.

So anyway, since then I have finally obtained my passport been taken out for dinner by a friend I met two years agoon a night bus home from a party. There was a couple having a huge argument next to us, we were opposite one another. We exchanged a few 'oh god look at these two!'looks. Eventually we decided to chat seeing as we were so uncomfortable about the two people next to us, and felt very put out at having to hear their personal life. We got off the bus at the same stop, kissed for a bit, exchanged numbers and been friends ever since! We have been friends since, but I have only actually seen him four times in two years. Knowing that I am fussy and how long we searched for a place with olives the previous time he took me out for a meal, I decided to cleverly purchase a bowl of mixed olives from M&S before going to the restaurant. I was therefore eating olives with chopsticks! Almost felt like hell, only jocking!!! It was a quirky challenge. We got on like a house on fire and talked openly about sex and previous partners. There was no shyness or awkwardness, and he even claimed that we would make a good couple.(I did not get the hint).

Walking me home I got an arm round my waist and a lovely waft of aftershave. Yes a manly grip and manly smell is always a good thing; even if it's out of fashion, there are natural instincts and testosterone is good at bringing them out. I'm glad to say that I seem to have more will power than I used to. (except last week) There was a long sturdy hug accompanied by a few kisses but no more.

Altogether quite pleased to be leaving the country.

I am currently on the train back from Brighton where I saw some great sites, tried to do some serious tourism, had fun and may have even re-invited a helper in France in exchange for French lessons.

When I arrived the plan was to go and see Arendul Castle, three men and me in a hired car. Full English breakfast was what we searched for on the way from Brighton to Arendul. After rejection from three restaurants we decided to just get to Arendul then eat and then find the castle. On arriving we found that the only day which the castle was not open to the public was clearly Saturday and resigned ourselves to breakfast in a tea room. Over tea, toast, bacon and eggs we came to the decision to see the cathedral instead and everyone including myself expected yet another mishap as we all concluded I was jinxed. We did none the less, climb through woods and got to the beach so all in all a fun filled day out slightly lacking in site seeing.

This was followed by karaoke on Brighton pier! It was a strange atmosphere, like a ferry boat lounge but full of people dressed as if in a night club all singing and dancing along to the music. It was fabulously tacky and the Spanish boys loved it. They all tried to sing along in English to a strange range of tacky classics, and when we all had lost our voices and the will to dance we headed back to the flat.

The sleeping arrangements turned out to be very comfortable, perhaps a little too comfortable. I was in bed with one man on either side of me, both snoring and letting out an incredible body heat! I noticed the next morning that men really do wake up with a hard on! Pierced in the back by one I decided coffee would be a good idea and got out of bed attempting not to wake either erect snorer. I made coffee for everyone, and mentioned nothing of the rude awaikeng. We went to the sea side that day threw stones and picked up shells which I hardly ever do and miss a lot. Relaxing has become a real treat and I can do it almost fully now.

Got back to London to pack late that morning, booked a taxi for the afternoon and slept a bit before heading to the airport. I stupidly phoned Mr N.S.R. before bed and actually ended up in tears. Partly due to nerves, emotion but mainly because he called me selfish. I hope that I am anything but selfish. I tell white lies and flirt alot, I am irrational and possibly unpredictable but I don't think I'm selfish.

You're a cold hearted warm blooded lover
You burn my body
You inflame my heart
But with your icy stare
You break me apart

You're a cold hearted warm blooded lover

You use my love
to keep you alive
drain me to sorrow
only to thrive

You're a cold hearted warm blooded lover

You freeze my soul
But burn with lust
I am out of control
I am lost

Anyway as I write now, I am on the flight, after having paid three times the cost of my flight in excess luggage and being searched because I forgot I had scissors in my hand luggage, but finally I am leaving the city and heading to my future in the remote foothills of the Pyrenees!

Here the hard work, determination, self control and logic will be put to the test. I am looking forward to blood, sweat and tears, because they can't effect anyone else and can only make me a better person.

Flying to a new world
Flying to a new me

𝓕𝓡𝓐𝓝𝓒𝓔 finally

<u>Day 1</u>

I got picked up from the airport by the caretaker, who said he was pleased to see me, because now someone could do the cooking and cleaning for him! Total cheek!!!Think he was kidding, but just on the off chance he was not I made sure he knew that that was not going to happen. I was shattered and wired with anticipation too, so went to bed late after doing the rounds of the house, writing some lists and calling family to let them know I had arrived safe.

It's pissing with rain and freezing cold but I did manage to sleep till two pm which I am a little pissed off about as I lost half the day but I did go straight out to till a small patch of earth at the front of the house. I am planning on planting a ton of vegetables, renovate the house and keep myself warm and alive. Using a pick axe without gloves inevitably gives you blisters. Building a fire big enough to heat the house because the heating isn't on inevitably gets you burnt and pulling up carpets, which are nailed and glued down with a pair of scissors, inevitably hurts your back. So I am in bed, in a little pain but ecstatic. The only thing I did do today which should have hurt and didn't, much to the surprise of my caretaker, was practise shooting for wild boar. I am determined to get one to make pâté and saussison but it means a large riffle and strong bullets. We practised in the rain, as the sun had almost set, on an old can of beans. The caretaker was surprised at how good I was and almost dismissed it as luck. He will be my only companion here and unfortunately is an insecure macho, ex womaniser who is good at cutting wood, playing the guitar, complaining and talking bollocks. He is a tall slim man aged 50+ who cares too much about his appearance and yet seems to do little about it. He likes to imagine himself as someone from his favourite westerns, he loves his horses, guns, saddles and women. Smoking his usual roll ups which he can somehow talk with in his mouth without them ever falling out, we discussed my plans for the house. He has good advise but also is very suspicious of everyone as well as being quite protective over me. "The cowboy" says I shouldn't tell the people around here any of my plans, hunt alone and be weary of anyone, needless to say he is very solitary, totally bloody paranoid, but he does like his women. He can't keep them long as either they bore him or they want more than a simple country life. He can and will however be a useful companion and easy to tease if ever I need a laugh. "The cowboy" has obviously had time to read a lot while being here and has a lot of knowledge and good conversation, though often he can go off on a tangent and exaggerate extraordinarily without shame! I am pleased to be here and listening to the rain outside fills me with calm bliss as I shut my eyes and await the alarm for the morning's work!

<u>Day 2</u>

Again slept in and was reluctant to get out of a warm bed. Had a boiling hot bath, cup of coffee which I had to filter by hand as the coffee machine has been chucked out. Rebuilt the fire from last nights embers and proceeded to smoke first roll up of the day.

When I finally found the scalpel and the strength to rip up the carpeting I got to work on the stairs then the bathroom, then the hall, then more stairs. Why was carpeting invented!!!

Now another problem, the wood under the toilet is rotten. So much so you can see right through to the TV below. I was horror stricken at how close any guest was to having fallen through to full view of any TV watchers below, while quietly and unsuspectingly taking a dump. Funny, yes it could be, but a real pain in the arse to fix after that! Not to mention damages and possibly being sued.

So "The cowboy" came over to give me some advise and actually ended up helping me rip out the toilet, saw off the rotten wood and break the TV in the process. A plank of wood inevitable fell directly on the television, but hey who needs T.V when you have so much to do, and plan and nature at your doorstep?. I have a few extra holes in my hands and a few more blisters but when I head to town tomorrow I will buy gloves as well as maybe getting the TV fixed, if there is time. It's been pissing down which makes the pick axe work far easier as the land is softer. Whacking away at the ground is also a brilliant stress relief. I did need this after finding another patch of rotten wood in the house this morning. This patch overlooks the corridor downstairs, where there's a grotto in the wall. We found it's existence recently when a panel of wall fell out to reveal this grotto. This alcove in the wall is used for wiring and is not lit. While looking down from the floor above into this alcove, it was so dark and difficult to make anything out. When my eyes adjusted I started to see objects and then my eyes fell on a persons head! A slightly ill looking head, lying back staring up at me.

I jumped back a meter with a screech a high loud scream. "The cowboy" had no idea what was wrong and seemed unphased when he looked down. Still with a high pitched panic in my voice; "Do you not see the guys head?" His answer was merely; "No it's a woman's head." How can that make any difference to the discovery of a bloody head in the wall? I was still shaking when he said "yes defiantly a woman why?" How was he so calm??

So clearly I ran down stairs to have a look and found, sitting on a chest in the corridor, a magazine with the picture of a woman on the front cover. Have calmed down since have smoked several rollies and drank a cup of extremely strong coffee. Not sure why I thought a dead body had been hidden in the wall, maybe I lack entertainment.

This evening "The cowboy" had a lady caller who stayed an hour and a half, needless to ask why someone would drive half an hour up a shitty road at night just to spend and hour and a half n someone's company.

I have not had too many lonely moments or thoughts about Mr N.S.R. except in my dreams obviously. I needed some contact with someone who knew him and what he was up to. So last evening I called my cousin to get some gossip. She was busy at work so she passed me onto my auntie who I had in fact been trying to call for two days. Mr

N.S.R. was beside her and clearly knew who was on the phone as my aunt said he was hovering, she did ask if I wanted to talk to him but ignored my negative answer and handed him the phone. I was quiet and a little put out and he initially thought I was sad. I tried tactfully to tell him I didn't want to talk to him, which worked better than I had expected. "Call me when you do have something to say then, ok, bye."

It's so nice that the mobile doesn't work here, and that I can speak to people if I want but that no-one is looking over my shoulder. I will however call some of the locals about to let them know I'm here and also look into a social job tomorrow in town. Can't totally become a hermit!

<u>Day 3</u>

Wow what a great day, again reluctant to get out of bed but managed before midday. Worked outside again in the rain but with gloves this time. Far less blisters, and a decent veg patch now on its way. I have not yet passed my driving licence, which in the middle of nowhere is pretty shit. I have to rely on 'The Cowboy' to drive me everywhere. Went to see "The cowboy" to ask about going to town and we both had forgotten it was November 11th, also a day of rest here and remembrance; no shops open in other words. "The cowboy" showed me an agricultural book, which I studies with great interest while his cat ate my laces. I was slowly creating a master plan of what to plant where, and how to make the house in to a running business. Also hope to be more and more self sufficient, chickens, vineyards, fruit trees, veg garden and maybe even a cow or something similar. So exciting!!! We talked of giving French/English lessons in which he would attend freely if he drove me there.

I've been moving boxes of my things around the house, moved the mattresses from my room to make place with my futon. Clearly, when we moved here from Scotland, my brother and sister chose their rooms first. My brother got first choice and chose my mother's, with sink, big bed and heating. My sister's has a view of the pool, a gorgeous box bed, sink and heating. Mine is the only other room with sink, it is bigger than theirs but, there are holes in the ceiling, which the cold air, rain and snow come through and most importantly no heating. It's at the very top of the house, so freezing in winter and boiling in summer, the worst but I love extremes. I have a sofa, two tables, double futon and multicoloured walls. I love it, it's far from the rest of the house and big enough for painting, dancing, exercise and sleeping. If I can renovate the rest of the house enough to rent, this space is perfect as a studio flat for me.

The TV has suddenly come back to life, which happened while it was unplugged. This scared me a little but I've been told that, if the antenna is in it's possible. Not sure I totally understand that but at least I don't have to think about getting it fixed.

I am fine here and have just phoned my old au-pair to come for lunch Saturday, then I plucked up the courage to phone an ex-boyfriend to see if not only he would come over but also give me advice on wine growing, farming and the legal procedures of a B&B here. I am already beginning to feel the solitude, but this is good for me, and I also think I had years of sleep deprivation to catch up on.

Ex/Farmer friend came over. He is a lovely big, dark and sweet guy with hands like shovels but a heart the size of an elephant. I was with him for four months, in which I realised that someone no matter how kind, who had not read nor been very scholarly in his life, couldn't keep my attention for very long. There was a time when I actually sat this lonely man down and said:-

"You know me, I've travelled and done a lot, you're best friend is your brother, you've never moved from here and you don't want to. You're not funny, not clever, not interested I'm anything but farming and not interested in sex, why am I with you?" Harsh I know but I needed to know that there was some passion there, there wasn't.

"Euh! Euh!" Was the only answer. If he had loved me he would have tried to keep me. Or maybe I went to far! Maybe we really weren't suited and he didn't feel the need to draw the experience out just for the sake of it.

None the less he stays a great friend whom I still find attractive and want to break out of his shell. I've tried already and failed, when I took him to Paris. He has now been to his first performance on stage, first fairground ride and first art gallery visit and first long train journey. This had very little effect on him. I tried to ask about his experience of Paris, hoping for wide eyed inspiration, but it falls on deaf ears as he admires the straightness of the vines on the way home on the train.

How could I take this natural, innocent happiness away from such a true symbol of honesty and kindness? He is probably a hundred times happier than me, in his simple life, not constantly in search of a challenge, not constantly putting pressure on himself to be a better person, not constantly trying to find better.

On a good day I feel blame,
On a bad one I feel the same
Come, come to me again
please ease the pain

I kneel to feel you whole
I crawl to have your touch
distorted relief to my soul
That is wrong for us so much

On a good day I feel sick
and I am slowly burning the wick
Fast and slow yet both ends quick

For the past hour I've been head banging to Meatloaf and singing to Michael Jackson, dancing for no reason and yet I am knackered from today's work. I am so looking forward to seeing some old friends, and very stupidly looking forward to seeing "shovel hands," while still thinking incessantly of Mr N.S.R..

Will send a message from town seeing as it's been three or four days since I've called, when in London I at least sent a text every day.

I have no idea if I am getting cynical about my love life, or I have just lost hope. I'm not going to stop liking love stories and romantic films but I should turn to agricultural and building manuals. I'm not likely to use any of my excessive passion, sex and love any time soon, and yet I don't want to loose my romantic edge even if I show a stony front. God shut up!!! You just need a good break from men in general!

I've written a long list of questions to ask "shovel hands" and his pal JaJa, I hope he will be a great help and confident in the years to come. I am going to try to become a farmer loving girl, who likes the simple things in life, and manual labour. There is something quite reassuring about a man who asks no questions and just gets on with it!

Actually, fuck all that, when I see an intelligent well read well spoken and well dressed anguished man I go weak. Give me an aristocrat rugby man anyday! (Watching Notting Hill, not helpful)

Day 4

Right, I managed to get up early, build a fire, tidy the house a bit and found loads of old photos. I love photos and memories, there were loads of my mum. Having old pictures of her is great because I've been using them as inspiration for painting in the past while getting pissed on cheap rosé in Paris. I induced depression in order to create, so many photos have gone astray in the midst of tears paint ans wine spilledge. I miss her a lot, and would really like to chat to her about my future sometimes. Obviously it hurts but feel her presence not only in the house but in me. When I sit at the table in the morning in her old green dressing gown and fag in hand I see her. There is nostalgic comfort in this. The vision of her before we came down for breakfast, her time, quiet before the three of us woke and brought mayhem to the house. These have become my times before anyone wakes (if the house is full) peace in the knowledge that there are friends close by, and yet quiet reflection until anyone comes.

Went to town today and realised I had lost my bank card. How do I do this! Passports, wallets, phones, now bank cards!!!! Have transferred some money but really will need to get a job. The Lino was three times the price I calculated it would be, so I have decided no heating, only cooking on the fire and recycle everything! Have almost cut down to no drink at all, had a pastice as an aperitif and then tea what a break through, going to bed sober and I actually love sitting up drinking tea and writing. Unfortunately the tea tastes of fish and cabbage as I used the same pan on the fire for both. I may have to invest in some pans too. I also may not have rinsed it properly after cooking so It's an interesting combination, of cabbagy/fishy tea that I positively don't recommend.

Received a letter from Mr N.S.R. today with a joints worth of hash in it which was a lovely surprise, and totally unexpected. Didn't know he would make the effort to actually write!He mentions how a lot is against us, and that there are a lot of differences of age, language and culture but also says that he wants to know me better and wishes he had made more of the time we had. Well all I can say is more fool you and if you won't come here to see me then its your loss not mine! I have plenty of other options. In fact I got a text from Art to day he was sorry he hadn't seen more of me in London. Again more fool him but he is more likely to come here than Mr N.S.R.. Art has a great way of organising his time, when he works, he works hard and when he plays work doesn't interfere. When I'm with him I really do feel like the centre of his attention, plus he is taller, bigger and more manly than Mr N.S.R. and therefore feels wonderful as an ego boost. I incidentally got a text from the "night bus" man asking how things were going. It's nice to know people care, seeing as they are both miles away they can't be just flattering me (I hope). Tomorrow is "The cowboys" birthday and ex-au-pair is coming with her extraordinary tall husband (she is small) and too quiet kids. I was baking a cake when the gas ran out but obviously at eight o'clock at night when the trip to town for the week had been done already! "The cowboy", much to his dislike, has agreed to go down tomorrow so I can cook a meal for us six and his present (the cake). He has gotten into a routine of going to town only once a week to save on petrol money. I understand this but have to say that my own company and his gets a bit dull after a few days.

Spoke to Shmona today too, which is always a joy and I have written her a letter too. I have a lighter heart after talking to her. Found so many photos of her here with me, by the pool with her long dark hair, pale skin and black swimming costume. Her eyes shine bright when she's here and her already huge white smile beams. When I talk to her about my days herez I know she understands the bliss better than anyone. The freezing cold wind and waves of sheet rain while at the top of the hill looking out to the valleys and mountains around is a feeling of pure awe and wonder that only she could truly share with me at this time. Never has anyone evoked and awoken my love of pure natural beauty, magic and passion. Not to mention she makes me laugh, inspires me to create and listens to my worries with real concern and great advice. Thank god for Shmona!

Day 5

Woke early and began frantically sweeping and cooking on the fire as I was unsure if "The cowboy" had gone to get gas, of course he had, but how could I have known. When he returned I had been boiling potatoes in the fireplace with not much luck and obviously burnt myself several times in the process. I managed to tidy cook and even have an aperitif ready by the time guests arrived, but not to cook the grattin enough. Trying to gage the heat level on an open fire is a skill I will have to develop if I want to cut costs of gas and electricity. Brigitte and her husband arrived just in the middle of my frantic cooking, frozen as it is really bloody cold here! She is a lovely small woman with short tinkerbell hair and huge deep dark eyes. What I really love is that she adored my mother, and was very grateful to have been employed by her for a year and a half, in Scotland, to look after us. She needed to get away from her life in France, and where further than the highlands. She always talks of her adventures there at my home and of my mother with the greatest zest and true admiration. I didn't know all the stories of personal trials and failed relationships that she witnessed while living with my mother. We were away at boarding school most of the time, and anyway too young for a mother to confide in. It is nice to have a perspective that confirms the humanity of people.

"The cowboy" joined us and we sat down to a very relaxed and simple meal which was greatly appreciated except for the undercooked grattin which I sneaked into "The cowboys" kitchen during desert (once it had cooked).That way he could cook it for his dinner on a real hob.

We had cake candles which was a great challenge on an open fireplace. I used two oven dishes to make a small oven type receptacle, that once heated I placed the cake into in a baking dish and it cooked the cake perfectly. I wrapped a few meagre gifts I found around the house in old cases and boxes, but they were thoroughly entertaining. I gave him two of those mind-bender puzzles that often one finds in stockings at Christmas. I have them but don't have the patience and determination that I'm sure he has in fact. I can see him now sitting up in bed with his glasses on the end of his nose, (which he is ashamed to wear most of the time as he is very vain) trying to figure one out just to prove to me that he can.

The kids joined in trying to decipher puzzles, playing games, dressing up etc. It was a joy to entertain them, and get to know the kids too. We had a good goggle. They have invited us over next Saturday which I am very pleased about but clearly "The cowboy" said immediately if there isn't an emergency or unexpected event. He has a slightly pessimistic outlook on life. I agreed immediately. Then the instructions were written for us on how to get to their house, so grumbles and mumbles of incomprehensible disapproval came from his direction. This is due mostly to the fact that he didn't have his glasses with him. We agreed finally to see them for lunch next week, with said drawn map.

Once they had left we got to work on replacing the rotten tiles in the toilets which was a pain in the arse. The main beam is squint and the new wood clearly not! This is going to be a problem throughout my renovations I am sure! Modern materials are straight, and often standard sized, whereas old houses are not. He taught me to saw without force, straight and with no splinters. (More complicated than one thinks)

We were both very proud of our work and I let him get to his grattin while I sanded the stairs. Now, I thought this would be easy. Bearing in mind I was pretty tired anyway from a day of entertaining and cooking without gas and fixing floor boards. I began at the bottom as it was getting dark and the upstairs lights aren't working.

I wrapped a huge pink scarf round my mouth and nose, got the electric drill with sander attachment and almost sent it flying four times. As soon as I hit the wood the drill flew to one side, the attachment flew out because I had not tightened it properly, and luckily it never hit my face in the process. Once I had got the hang of it it was dusty and lengthy, the glue must have been caked on. In an hour of sanding I can see the wood now on only two steps! Grand total of two from thirty, not too impressive but I want to do it right, anyway the wax and varnish are the wrong colour and I can't change them till Monday so I have time.

I tried to call Mr N.S.R. as there was a call last night just after midnight, when I was in bed writing. As I ran down to the phone I tripped over the dinning room chair and fumbled for the study light but, alas, not in time. Obviously just as I got to bed it rang again so this time I took the quicker route, but this means more obstacles, and I still missed the call, but really hurt my toes too. The quicker route was not quicker and has caused a bruise on my shin and the call was missed again, so went to bed a little more pissed off than the first time.

Anyway he didn't answer, not really surprising considering our last conversation, and it is a Saturday night, if he's not working he's probably out having fun, good for him! All in all not a very productive day for the house but at least "The cowboy" had a proper birthday celebration, I saw some close friends and the toilet will be back to functional. I can quickly fix the room up repaint and have a bath again. In this heat or lack of, a steaming bath can never go amiss! I've only gone 3 days without and it's quite enough. My bath, my bath, my kingdom for a steaming, perfumed bubble bath!

Unbelievable, truly unbelievable, the same exact thing has happened again. The phone rang a few moments ago, it is two am!! I ran, stumbled, fumbled, froze and missed the call! SO ANGRY! Will try tomorrow during the day though I'm sure he won't be up till 5pm at the earliest.

Day 6

Trouble getting out of bed again today, not fucking surprising its bloody snowing! Anyway, first thing I did was to replace the toilet (heavy) and screw it into the new floorboards. Clearly there is a leak, which inevitably leaked onto the TV again and fused it again. Decided to go for a walk in the wind and snow to send a text to Mr N.S.R. and possibly collect mushrooms. Anything to get me out of the house, and the terrible mess I am making of fixing the plumbing. I went across to let "The cowboy" know and also to check who the call at 2 am was from. He had assumed it was from my sister seeing as it was a Spanish number. He asked me to have a look out for wild boar footprints so that we could go hunting, cool!!!. I really want to get one, so I can make it into pâté and even have my first wild boar trophy head! Well maybe not that could be a bit gross, but hey a warm wild boar stew in this snowy weather wouldn't go amiss! Hehe.

My walk was a lot shorter than planned and the wind and snow was far colder and harsher than I had anticipated. I collected two handfuls of mushrooms that seem only to grow in cow pats or horse turds! Got a bit of kindling for the fire and headed home with my fingers actually physically aching from the cold. When I got in I placed myself in front of the fire in a vain attempt to relieve the pain but seriously to no avail for at least ten minutes. I didn't realise frostbite exists in Europe!!I have a high pain tolerance, but finger tips are full of nerves, and they were excruciatingly painful. As the tears of pain rose to my eyes I decided to run them under hot water. I know and knew I was wrong but I was desperate. I felt like someone was hammering nails into the ends of every finger under the nail. Clearly if you know anything about chillblanes etc. never go straight from hot to cold!!

Once the pain had subsided I tried to sand some more stairs, and then went to let "The cowboy" know that the toilet was still leaking and that I would need a hand moving it again and finding the leak. He also showed me that I had to put a lot more pressure on the sander when sanding and sanded a step and a half to the extent they should be. This clearly means that the two steps I was so proud of yesterday don't look like they have even been touched! I will be there for weeks, months maybe years! It's ok I have weeks.

Phoned a Scottish friend near by who will be coming for dinner Tuesday and hopefully bringing me some smoking material. He is a bit hippy and has a bike, beard and dreaded blond hair. We get on very well considering I have only seen him a few times at family parties and then last summer twice when I discovered he was living near here. Originally his parents would drag him and his sister to parties at our house and vice versa, we didn't have much in common at the time and sometimes even dreaded it. Now both living in the middle of nowhere in France, we suddenly have much more in common, and old stories to recount.

Also phoned Mr N.S.R. which was a good thing, even though he had replied to my text after I had got back out of reception's reach to tell me to phone after nine, which I did not. I phoned at 7ish so he clearly was at work and couldn't talk long, good for me as the study is freezing, I was even wearing a winter hat and scarf while on the phone (indoors!). I have had to come to terms with the fact that he isn't ever going to come here to see me, but none the less it's nice to think of someone who may be thinking of you. It's comforting to think you matter to someone.

I am not going to concentrate on him or any other love affair until I have a serious work plan, a job and a notion of where I will be mentally and financially in 3 months time. I haven't actually been very awake since I've been here, although I have done some hard work on the house I have found myself sitting beside the fire, smoking and not only doing nothing but thinking nothing, or just being numb. It's relaxing but it doesn't get anything done does it, and I don't feel great abpout myself when I'm in that state. Money is going to be a huge problem seeing as I have managed to loose my bank card already, can't get work till after Christmas, if I can get work at all. I have to get to Spain for Christmas to see the family and all the renovation material is costing more than expected. Oh well at least I can say one thing, without doubt, I am not bored and busy but relaxed. I hope it stops snowing and raining as we have to chop more wood for the months to come. Otherwise I will be in winter gear inside from now til Spring.

It's been a week!
Day 7

Woke up with the worst head ache ever so stayed in bed looking out of the window in wonder at a sunny day I was wasting! Motivated myself to move eventually.

Showered, changed went next door to "The cowboys" with my coffee in hand and smoked one of his horrific roll-ups. I persuaded him to let me use the strimmer to cut down the brambles where I was going to plant my vegetables. He explained that the last two dogs and the cat had been buried out there, which gave my insides a jerk. I thought it through and thought that seeing as we had been talking of the natural cycle of the world. In a comprehensive and not sarcastic way; I said that they would give a better taste to the veg as it would be fertiliser. I was determined not to let his pessimism and negativity get to me, or change my big plans.

We went out him with a chainsaw, me with a scythe and started to chop what we could. This was taking forever, and using a scythe is so tiring for very little result! The easiest way to get rid of all the brambles in one go would be the strimmer. I begged and insisted, eventually I had a pair of straps over my shoulders and a strimmer hanging from my waist. "The cowboy" was surprised at how quickly I picked it up. You swish from left to right, try to ignore the thorns and pieces of wood that fly at you and try to cut as close to the ground as possible. Not rocket science, but admittedly can be harder than it looks, and dangerous too. The problem is that if you are amidst the brambles the strimmer gets caught but seeing as its strapped to you it's very difficult to get untangled. There's a method of strimming and pushing all the debris to the side as you go, this demands a lot of energy and coordination. God knows how Prince Charming got to the sleeping beauty without killing himself and all he had was a sword!

Anyway got it all eventually done and "The cowboy" actually congratulated me, he was truly impressed and shifted the strimmed bushes with a pitch fork in the dimming sunlight.

I then decided that it was not enough work for a lazy cunt who got out of bed at 2.30pm so as the sun set in my gloves and hat, scythe in hand I started on the pond, which had been overrun with weeds and small trees. I was half hoping that shovel hands an JaJa would turn up just then, not only to see me at work (proving I could) but to give me a good excuse to stop for a drink. I did eventually stop, my fingers were frozen and I was working by moonlight and the reflection from the house lights. It was beautiful, and strangely serene. As I realised there would be no guests tonight I began on the stairs again. I have now realised that they really will take me a month to do, but that's fine I have years!

I have been laughing, smiling and being generally calmer and happier than in a long time. The fruits of this move are starting to show. I even sat to a painting tonight, with half a beer and a joint(seeing as I had been sent it) I managed to begin on a canvas I made myself six months ago, so clearly it's not so stretched any more but well, hey, never mind. It is creativity after all!

Right going to sleep now so I can at least get something productive done before going to town tomorrow.

PS down to 5 cigarettes a day rather than 40, exercising everyday, and drinking far less!!!

Day 8

Can't believe I'm so happy, sane and pretty much healthier. Dug up some of the pond today it's bloody ridiculous. There's cement or some other type of rock hard material on the bottom! (Rock maybe). Anyway it's impossible to shift. Defeated by the pond, I decided to take my energy to another activity essential to the renovation of and old farm house. I've been cleaning, not like me I know, but I have. Went shopping for a new joint for the toilet and to change the colour of the varnish for the floor and stairs. I had the wrong varnish, and want to sand the floors and doors then varnish both in a matching lovely mahogany colour.

Have been sanding again and spending hours on the fucker! I am in agony, blisters, cuts and muscle aches in my arms! I really just want to set it all on fire, but that would only make the house colder than it is already.

Clearly Mr N.S.R. called while hippy man was here for dinner. It was not a good timing he said that he has no luck, and sounded genuinely upset as we have not spoken for days now. I told him I'd call back after hippy man had left. By the time he had left, which was not late I was far too stoned to have a conversation with anyone let along in Spanish so I got an earful the next day. I can't cope with your social life, who was it, where are they from, I'm not there! Etc etc. So I feel no guilt as he could be here if he had wanted to be. He does not work all the time, and spends more than he earns anyway in bars. It also means he cares at least and hopefully is not doing anything with any other drunken lost soul. (Which I am no longer, but was when we met!!!)

Stoned, going to write this properly tomorrow. P.S. it's getting slowly colder and it's going get worse according to the weather forecast.

So much so that "The Cowboy" told me we can't get out for a month at a time here in winter! If there is that much snow I'm gonna make the most of it and get the skis out!! Or my sisters snowboard! She never uses it now that she has her family life on the beach in Spin, not much snow there. Can't wait to get on the slopes!

Day 9

Today I put the Lino down after having wrapped all the stocking presents for the family. I know it's early but it cheered me up and when I don't write a plan out I don't know what to do in a day. I may be a bit more depressed than I originally thought

Today was great though, we fixed the new rotten bit of floor board that "The Cowboy" almost went straight through when putting the toilet back in place. We then went hunting but when I spotted a dear he wouldn't let me shoot it, he's a lot more sensitive than I thought. But then I found out years later that dear were off limits in my village because one of the ladies here had tamed one once, so no one can shoot them in case it's that dear. I will get a boar before Christmas. I will!!

I am getting into old routines, bad ones and I need to get a grip, write lists and give myself goals and restrictions otherwise my health and mentality will suffer. Think Positive Tabby! Plan future, look forward not backwards! etc etc

Day 10 (crossed out) 11

Put the rest of the Lino down, put my futon together and went to town via a friend of "The cowboy." She has been building her house for 20 years and it looks great, was very inspirational to me, and made my project a plausible goal rather than a crazy ass venture. There's hope for me!!! She had contacts for me, teachers and official addressed for me to look into teaching English as a backup income. She also suggested an artist who may be interesting in exhibiting my pictures!

When I got home I decided for some reason, best known to a mental and eccentric preadolescent, to papier mâchée the bath! No no really its great, and a cheap, but not very water proof way of doing it, so have varnished it too!!! It will eventually look like a lagoon or pond in a forest. I am also going to paint the walls as a forest. How exciting I'll have a forest in the house with a hot spring (shut up you freak!).

I was almost in tears today while driving home. The colours in autumn here are amazing, the vineyards can be green, yellow, bright orange or burgundy deep and rich. The sheer beauty of the fields of fire and the trees with flames falling and blowing in the wind brought me to tears! What is wrong with me? How are such small details making me emotional?!

It was truly incredible and proof of a greater force of nature. I think I'm getting sentimental or maybe I am drinking too much water at the moment and it is coming out of my eyes. I AM SO HAPPY HERE!I also have seen a future version of my work, and also potentially have contacts for earning an income.

Phoned my aunt this evening to check on her, my cousin and pregnant sis. My cousin has stress and high blood pressure, my aunt has an infection in her jaw and gums and some problem I've never understood in her hand. My sister, well she's about to give birth. I'm assuming that that's quite stressful too. It was maybe not the most refreshing conversation, but maybe I can look at my life now and think' well this is better than some'.or is it?

My aunt is very happy for me as I sound happy and told her all I was up to. When she coughs on the phone it's just as if I'm talking to my mother. It goes on for ages, and you can't get a word in, just have to wait til it passes and carry on the conversation from where it left off, if you can remember. They have the same voice and now my aunt has picked up gestures that my mother did. Maybe I just notice them more because I don't have my mother in front to compare them with anymore. It's nice to have such vivid reminders of the person who's been the most important in your life so far. I often want to call her and tell her what I am up to, and get her advice when things are not going like I hoped.

Anyway, today was inspiring and so much so that the bathroom doesn't look too bad, I feel fab and have loads of new plans for the house, teaching and getting on just fine here.

<u>Day 10 (crossed out) 12</u>

Great day out to Brigitte's, the old au-pair we had, in her new house. Got up pretty early too and managed to tidy a bit, finish off doing the Lino and found that the fucking toilet is still leaking! How is it possible? After fixing it twice? I just don't get it!! It's mathematically impossible, well only if we got everything absolutely right. Tomorrow I will start to do some real work and get up early, have to stop thinking about sex, love, nature and else, I need to get to work and lose all this weight I put on in London, now that I'm in a good frame of mind.

Sis phoned(actually no, I called her obviously), she was very nice to me so she must have got a call from my auntie or "The cowboy". She said she was proud of me which was meant sincerely! Anyway I'm knackered and need to get up early to begin my healthy happy routine!!

<u>Day 13</u>

Fucked up majorly on the routine but did get up at 8.30, walked and saw the neighbours. I asked them for shit, I know it sounds stupid but they have cows. It seemed logical that way would have spare fertiliser for my garden. It was the most beautiful day; warm, sunny, not a cloud or flake of snow in sight! I learned to use a chainsaw, how to start it, file it, check fuel and chain oil, and be safe. There are 20 hectares of wood here, and that also is a good source of income, so learning this skill will be helpful for money and essential for survival in the cold. I was so pleased with myself I even tidied away a box full of random cassettes, sorted old paper work and studied a bit more agriculture. The cassettes were a strange mix from childhood recordings to box sets of my mother's. They are all either in their original boxes or recognisable for what they are, but sorting them into; genre, working or not and empty cases took hours. I really have had a wonderful day but the drinking has not gone away and even though I have no wine in I managed to drink half a bottle of martini tonight! I can't let depression take over me again, this move is the best idea ever!!!Really need to get a grip. Find the right routine shitface!!!

Day 12

Today was brilliant sunny and not too cold. I got up early wrote a plan for the day, which I almost entirely stuck to, and even used the chainsaw again (liking this), piled wood on the tractor and have found a quick way to pay for my driving lessons and test. Sell wood by the ton, from the Forrest! It's around 100€ per ton so if I sell five I should be fine! What a great idea "The cowboy" came up with.(He has been selling our wood behind our backs for years, No doubt the way he can afford expensive cars etc.)

I saw myself in ten years time, driving the same rickety orange tractor with a 13 year old niece on the side being bounced up and down as I drive. Her grinning and chattering away, me explaining how to correctly cut from the woods, and all sorts of other useful information. I do see myself here and making it work, it's just going to take time!

I have managed to entirely burn my upper lip! I was cooking a piece of sausage on the end of my fork on the fire, when I went to eat it I heard a sizzling sound before realising the fork had scorched four lines into my top lip. I'm pleased it's that rather than a chainsaw or tractor accident. But this just shows how impatient and maybe reckless I can be.

I had a very peculiar dream last night in which I actually tested myself on general knowledge. I had to answer too. What is the name of the group of beings with eight legs? 'Octopede' well, when I awoke I had forgotten the answer but remembered the question. I asked "The cowboy" who told me I was a strange one, asking myself such questions while asleep. Just at that point I remembered 'octopede'!!!Yes Octopede!!! Which to me sounded like a made up word but logical, you know when you say a word too often and repeat it over and over it just starts to sound ridiculous. To "The cowboy" it was the most ridiculous and funny thing he'd ever heard. BUT, haha, I looked the word up and not only does it exist, it means a creature with eight legs. (Small pleasures).BIG GRIN

Goodnight world, gonna dream of wild boars, ex boyfriends and wild sex which seems recurrent in my dreams at the moment.

<u>(Actually its day 14)Confused days the other night due to Martini!</u>

Got up at 9am which was lovely with heating now, as I have the boiler working, and a hot water bottle. The heating had not been turned on that was all, but the fuel may run out, so I may have to order more! YET ANOTHER Cost!!! There was less problems with getting out of bed. I had yet again had a sexual dream. I had a quick coffee and began to paint the landing. The paint which I found in the tools shed, was not open and clearly indicated on the can that it was white It actually turned out to be a deep salmon pink, too offensive for 9.30 in the morning. OH shit, well what the hell will I paint this colour!???AGH!!!I needed to repaint the landing, and the light was very dim at the moment anyway as the lamps are not ll working, so safe enough for SALMON PINK. As I painted I had the firm notion in my head that I would re-paint it all white again when I finally <u>bought</u> some paint. Why carry on painting you may well ask. Well, I just felt like it and persuaded myself that an extra coat of paint could do no harm. It looks ok so have kept it that way.

While painting I heard "The cowboy" stating up the tractor. Haha another session of chopping and piling tree trunks. I ran downstairs, obviously spraying pink paint all over the newly waxed and stained flooring, to make sure I wasn't left behind. He was at the door ready to knock as I opened. We were off to chop down an old and dying fir tree, but we would go to the woods in the afternoon. "The cowboy" sniggered at my eagerness, as he has never seen a woman doing a man's job with any joy before.

We took a few photos of me wearing a beret, driving the tractor and chain sawing parts of a tree, as proof of my exploits. It was before facebook days, and even internet at the house so no remaining proof.

I then got back to my painting, and when I finished decided to sand the paint off the doors to stain them the same colour as the floor, a deep mahogany. As I sanded with all my weight pressed against the electric sander, an image began to appear. The white paint I had been sanding was clearly a second coat. The layer bellow was a dark grey shade. There wasn't a painting or picture underneath, but the effect of sanding in areas harder than in others, meant that where I hadn't got through to the wood, there was a shading effect. A face began to come to me so I just enhanced it by sanding lightly where I wanted shade, or dark areas and sanding right to the wood for the contours of the image. I was brilliant, I had created a slightly demonic face protruding from a door seemingly on fire! Strangely enough this face actually resembles my late father, and I have a feeling he was watching me waiting to be discovered!

When "the cowboy" came back I was still sanding. I didn't hear him so he went off to the woods without me. I therefore walked there and followed the sound of the chainsaw to find him.

I was absolutely knackered by the third log I hauled onto the back of the tractor. I was enjoying it but finding each one more and more of a struggle, I kept dropping them, or not throwing far enough for them to actually land on the pile. I eventually picked one up with one hand at either end, realising it was too heavy I thrust it towards myself and bent my knees so that I wouldn't drop it! Not a great plan, as the log had a sawn off branch protruding from the side and thrust at my crotch. Ow! Yes you can say that again and twice if your a bloke! I clearly dropped the bastard and held my wounded parts. It is going to take a lot longer than a week to make me into a real woodchuck self sufficient farmer girl! "The cowboy" who had finished sawing ran to my rescue, not sure of what had happened and promptly burst into hysteria when he realised. Not helpful, and I honestly wanted to belt him round the head with a log, but I will have to work up to that.

Not sure why, but as I write I just thought, "what if I die now?" "Will someone sell my door for millions?" What a total freak I am, really!But maybe they will!!!

Where was I, oh well anyway it was hell getting out of the woods as they are now damp from all the rain earlier last week. The tractor span and skidded but "The cowboy" seems to be very used to this, I on the other hand was seriously shitting my pants. I was sat on the side, above the back wheel and permanently thought I was going to be ejected or that we would topple over. There is no cabin on the tractor, just an old open sit-on tractor.

I was so proud of my sanding/creation that decided later to try to put an elf type figure on the top half of the door. When I had finished

I sprinted straight to "The cowboy's" house to get his opinion. He was flabbergasted, he loved it and clearly the nymph pleased him more than a little. She was naked. Men! But I am pleased that the renovating has also been creative. I am now totally pooped and will no doubt sleep like a log! One of those huge heavy mossy logs I have become so obsessed with!

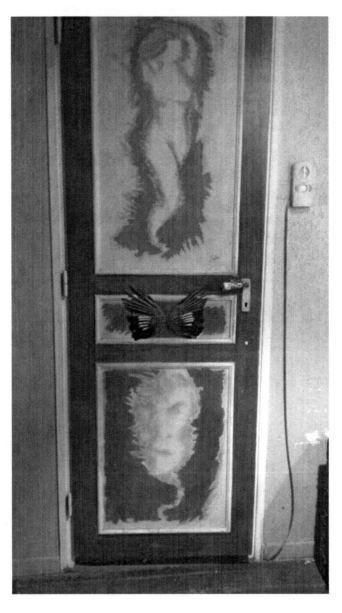

<u>Day 15</u>

Now confused more than ever, it's 12.25am and Shovel hands has just left. We chatted about what I need to know about agriculture about the future the past and friends. He looks at me with pride and respect, I love it, but he is far too shy to say anything compromising, or from the heart. I don't want him to either as I know it would not last long between us(tried before) and he is a great friend. I would love for him to do something out of character, for his sake. He dares to touch my hand longer than normal and looks straight into my eyes with a held gaze which is slightly unnerving, but that is all.

On another note, earlier today, I have made the sink and bedey into trees and begun to put flowers, made of small hexagonal marble tiles on the walls. The bathroom looks more and more like a forest and I am relaxed, a little confused and ready for bed.

<u>Day 16</u>

Heard noises in the night and was even persuaded I could hear someone in the house. It is an old house, and I am alone in it far away from any neighbour. I persuaded myself to go back to sleep after calculating exactly what I would do, where I would hide and what weapon I would use if indeed there was an intruder in the house. I woke fine though and the sun shone with no wind for the first time since I've been here. The day could have been an August summers morn. I've spent this morning hammering sanding and gluing wood together to make shelves. These are for the bathroom as they are made of pine trunks and go very well with the forest theme. I have put pine cones on the door and painted the trunks on the toilet and sink in brown.

"The cowboy" came round, we walked and talked in the sun. I whistled through a blade of grass and the madness started. The horse went mental and galloped around huffing. She got out of her pen and ran up the hill!!So we slowly concocted a plan to lure her back in with a bowl of grain, and someone sneaking behind with a stick to make sure she didn't bolt away again.

After succesfully getting the horse back in the pen, "The cowboy" and I began to make strange animal noises and even began walking around like monkeys. I think the constant wind had gotten to us, and this was the first day without! We were in hysterics, and then he said, "right let's have a competition!"

He is the type of person who loves to show off so clearly I was sure this would involve something he was good at. A shooting competition! Brilliant, but I warned him, half meaning it, that he wasn't allowed to get grumpy if I won. He hadn't even contemplated the thought. I drew two sets of targets for us while he went to get the riffle and bullets. I'd forgotten how much I loved the sport. We shot eight rounds each with a visor, which makes you see further but also makes you more aware of how much you shake. It took me two shots to get used to this. I also have a drawback; I am right handed with an astigmatism in my right eye. I therefore place my head over the riffle and look through my left eye. This looks very uncomfortable to a bystander, but I have gotten used to this unconventional method. I unfortunately won this amicable competition but was put in my place as "The cowboy" explained that there were other ways of shooting that I could never do, as well as many quick draw strategies that he would beat me at with his eyes closed. Luckily I am very good at flattering him, so clearly asked him all the right questions to allow him to go off on a tangent about his past successes. Phiew! childish tantrum avoided.

I phoned Mr N.S.R. this evening feeling half guilty for not having called in ages but also for having been so affected by Shovel hand's visit last night. He was pissed and adamant that I should know how much he loved me and wanted to see me. To say he was repetitive and very enthusiastic would be to say that being taken to accident and emergency, then the maternity ward by my mother, to give birth to a deodorant can lid, was a little embarrassing (I will allude to this event in more detail when it is more relevant).IE massive understatement!!

Anyway, the conversation was very romantic and at least I know that I will see him for most of my week in Spain. He says he has a mission to make me fall in love with him and that he regrets not having made the most of the time we had together when I was last in Spain. Hindsight!!!is a bitch

I know me, and I know I will battle against falling totally him, which should be fairly easy considering I will only be there a week and have this paradise to come back to. I really am fine here and so much happier than I could have imagined. I don't suppose it will last forever or be everyday but I have made a decision and I have every hope and belief it will all go well. I am worried that Mr N.S.R. has a trick up his sleeve, and that my autonomy will be at risk but I am also sure of one thing. I am really doing a good job here and even though I fall in love easily (or at least get attached)I will have less reason to now. The need for companionship is huge, probably due to the loss of my parents, but here I feel great alone! I am no longer looking. Also this may give him the notion of coming here, which would be great for a short time. Once he sees the way I live, how happy I am here and how bad I smell, he'll change his mind. A far cry from the trapping of Spanish beach resorts and night clubs.

Day 17

Have a strange friend of my mother's here who has decided to stay the night. He is going through a nervous break down, sexual problems with his wife and general depression which I have been subjected to for six hours continuously. He is on a strange diet consisting of veg and protein powder which he forgot to bring so he's been in complete turmoil. He told me, without asking first, that he was staying the night and intended to help out in the morning and I have now realised how invasive people are now that I'm used to my solitude.

Ground breaking news, and completely out of the blue!!!!The greatest thing has happened today!!!! I am being given two pregnant goats!! Given, yes by a friend of "The cowboy" who makes cheese from the milk and is a very lovely man! Of course he is, he's giving me two goats!!

Day 18/9

Trying to get to sleep was impossible last night. Mr Busybody was moving furniture around and had got me so worked up that I was worrying all night. How to finish the bathroom, how to build a goat pen, how to manage the births, how to milk goats and feed the kids at the same time. What would I feed them? What would I feed myself? How did I know how to make cheese? Etc etc, all with a slightly pessimistic tone. When I woke I lit the fire and rushed to have a quiet coffee before Mr BB came down. A moment of pure bliss before he manically came down, asking about the coffee, whether the water had been filtered beforehand, whether the coffee had been in an airtight package, etcetc. He was going to take me to the two properties nearby that he was trying to sell. He had no idea, with all his excitement and enthusiasm that I was completely indifferent about this venture. We had an hour before we were expected at the first property so, he instructed me to get on with my chores while he amused himself. I at the point put my foot down and said very amicably "as long as you don't rummage around the entire house!" He got the message and went over to see "The cowboy" instead, poor him.

We finally set off once Mr BB had located his computer, his mobile, his hands free set, his car keys, his hat, his gloves etc. He has an amazing nack of stressing me out and pushing my patience. The first property was owned by a horseman friend of "The cowboy" whom I had met on several occasions on his rides here. This long grey haired, bearded man owns a house and land not far from here over looking a vineyard. The interior was astonishing, all wood and white plaster with guns and swords hanging on the walls. The plaster had a type of Gaudi effect and made the whole place look like a cave. The Mexican drapes and guitar added to the Spanish tavern look. It was beautiful and he was a brilliant host. I and Mr BB sat at his bar type construction and shared a glass of port with him. Mr BB only had a sip due to his obscure diet. I discovered that this traveller had also been given goats by the same man who has offered me goats. He said they were great company, easy to look after and produced excellent milk. I hope this is true!!!!I can't wait!!!yeah!!!! Mr BB who is less than interested in country life quickly butted in with "shall I just leave you two here then to get pissed and talk about goats?" How rude, just because he had something that we both wanted to talk about and were interested in!

Eventually we headed off to the second property which was an organic oil and perfume factory. We met the owner who was a very attractive tall dark man with slightly camp or precious mannerisms. We went to his shop to smell the essential oils and perfumes, and this was just incredible. He explained how the cents were made by collected and extracting the oil from which ever plant it was. I felt like I was back at school in a chemistry class, but this was fascinating. It was interesting to find out what scents procure what sensation, or cure what ailment. Mr BB was looking for anti-viral aids and something for his daughter's itchy skin. He had, needless to say, looked up all possible antidotes on the Internet and plummeted the host with endless quetions. The owner was at a loss after ten minutes of Mr BB's rantings and interruptions. I did my best to keep the air clear and comical dispute the fumes of rosemary musk and eucalyptus. In the end Mr BB has exasperated the poor man, who decided to let BB come to his own conclusions, and made some excuse about having to get back to work.

On the drive home Mr BB commented on what a good choice my father had made in choosing this house for peace and quiet. I was at this point a little less subtle and explained in a bit too much detail what pleasure there was in not being bothered by anyone. He got the message and after dropping me home made his excuses and headed home to Toulouse. Phiew, what a relief! He is a lovely kind hearted man, but after twenty four hours I was ready to shoot him and pull all my hair out!

I was drained! More so than after chopping wood and sanding all day, or even a seven hour trek. It was incredible how much energy it had taken to stay calm, concentrate on his ranting and not blow a fuse. I went over to check how "The cowboy" was as he had been accosted by Mr BB just before he left that morning.

We had a lot of common complaints to share and were both drained of strength and pushed to the point of explosion. Luckily we turned to practical issues such as the goats and the natural water source for the house. This, I knew existed but had never seen it. So we went out in the rain to discover an ancient cove in the mountain side while alluding to our favourite French novels. "Jean de Florrette" and "Manon des sources." I could at this point feel the rain turn slowly to sleet and fall slower. Sleet and snow are blown by the wind while rain falls fast and directly down due to it's density. AGH!!! this is sleet!!!We found the entrance to the cove overgrown with brambles, which meant I would have to come back with a strimmer. I insisted on checking if there was water flowing out of it at least, in the pipes heading to the house. There was! This will be essential for watering the vegetables, and providing water for the goats, and maybe chickens one day soon.

It is now a few hours later and there is real snow, thick and soft which I think will settle.

I really hope it doesn't settle because the road is fairly bad and usually un drivable in the snow. I love it here but, having the choice to leave when I want or even having guests come visit, taken away is more than irritating. I do have a lot to keep me busy, and plenty of meditating on my future to do. Time alone is really helping me put my life back into perspective but I am looking forward to Christmas with friends and family.

Day 20

Yesterday we had to go to town for "the cowboy" to get a mole removed. He is hilarious, the façade of the big macho woodchuck is absolutely transparent to me. He pretends he is tough, but he was terrified of a knife coming anywhere near him!! He even picked me up and kissed my cheek when we left, proof of how scared he really had been.

Did some plastering of walls and evil blocking of mouse holes in the hope that they will die of claustrophobia. The kitchen walls were crumbling in several places, and obviously the mice decided it was a perfect motorway to the food cupboard. Again drained of energy after a day's work, but also maybe the cold weather.

"The cowboy" and I sat in the evening listening to old French music playing the guitar and he even persuaded me to sing. Yet again I surprised him, he was very complimentary which I coolly appreciated and accepted.

Today was frosty and we had to go back down to pay an electricity bill I had overlooked. They were about to cut the electricity off! I can tell you that would have been a monumental pain in the rear!

I wall papered the downstairs bathroom with old newspaper clippings of my fathers. He had in one of his eccentric whims funded a small ballet company which he lost a lot of money on but kept all the reviews. The walls are now an array of black and white photos, dancers and eight mm film reels. I then varnished the whole lot to avoid the dampness from the shower to unstick or damage the paper.

Seeing as it is the first of December I went out with an axe this evening to chop myself a Christmas tree!!!!Even though the family isn't here, and I have no children I am going to decorate and listen to carols till Spain to get me in the mood. There is so much nostalgia about Christmas. I axed the tree, because I wanted to deserve it, not just get 'The cowboy' to chainsaw it down. Without a word I walked into the woods, in the freezing cold and began to chop away at what looked like a reasonably sized tree that was almost straight.

Mr N.S.R. was very suspicious of my free gifts of goats, horses and cats. In his world, nothing comes for free, I know this to be true for most people but they unfortunately think in material terms. I plan to repay these kind neighbours, obviously, in my own way. I can give them jams and cheeses regularly once I start making it. I can also give them eggs, or offer help on their farms. I think I may have found someone who is trying to get rid of their rabbit hutches and also has a van he is willing to transport my new goats in. It's all very exciting, and happening very fast. All it takes it's to ask, for a favour, and if they say no well, find someone else. Not everyone is as honest as that though are they?

Mr N.S.R. was also concerned about Mr Busybodie's visit and asked me what he had wanted. I actually couldn't reply as I really have no idea, maybe to release some pent up stress, get away from his wife for a bit or just wanted to snoop around and rant at me, I'm just pleased it only lasted a day!I honestly did not mind that much anyway, he is and will be a good help for my plans here. He knows the house well, and even much of the electrical and plumbing systems here.

I now understand the term worship the wind, it is howling today but the broken silence and sheer power of nature give me strength. The horse has been galloping wildly and all the neighbours goats and sheep are going wild! Nature's response to the change of temperature and season is infectious, and I love it.

The lightest heavy heart
Floating but always down
Lost in purpose and direction
Torn apart by temptation

The loss of control is not new
yet my soul never strengthens with time
the control that I've lost in you
Will slowly succumb to be mine
The lightest heavy heart
Floating around and around
Lost in purpose and direction
scared of its own reflection
who do we have to hide from now
no mirrors or lights underground
hiding from the pressure to win
we could bury ourselves in our sin
The lightest heavy heart
floating about in the wind
searching for a real purpose
wanting a life and yet nervous
Free me into the wilderness
enfold me, break me with kindness
the breath of freedom is kisses
and yours is what my heart misses
The lightest heavy heart
floating in your direction
frustrated that we are apart
missing your perfect erection

<u>Day 21</u>

What a day! We built the goat's pen, which really surprised "The cowboy." He was shocked at my strength and my rapidity at learning new skills. I was very proud of myself, as we have built, a 4 by 10 meters' pen, and two small shanty huts for them to shelter under. It really does look a bit like a shanty town, but I am sure they will be very happy there. Yipee, good job, nailing planks together, wiring fencing together, making doors, and roofs, I am so pleased!!!I think I may be ok being a burly farmer person after all!

'The Cowboy' also took the complete piss out of me for taking the wrong tool to chop the Christmas tree. I had in my hurry picked up the yellow handled hammer type thing rather than the similarly yellow handled axe type thing. They look the same, and a sledge hammer also has a pointier end, just not as pointy! It had taken me ages but I had none the less managed to chop it and drag it back to the house, through the forest. It did take me an hour to push the fucker up the stairs to the big open room that used to be the barn. I didn't realise the size of it until I got it home, it looked so small in the forest compared to the other trees!! It touched the ceiling which is about 5meters high, actually the end is a little bent, so no fairy on top. The tree has now lights on it and one solitary ball on it for the moment. The one ball is to mark the occasion, but I was so knackered after dragging it in, getting it upright, while having spikes in my arms and tangled in my hair that one ball was all the strength I could muster.

We shifted some more wood that afternoon, and piled it safely in the woodshed. We then had a coffee while I played him the original of an Ertha Kitt song I had sung to him the night before.

As I prepared dinner "The cowboy" came over, I had been screeching to a carol CD to put me in the Christmas mood. I thought he had come over worried that I was yelling or hurt I was a little embarrassed. When I saw the sheepish look on his face I realised something had happened. He was truly scared when he announced that his friend had offered him two horses rather than one, the second being a small female for me. He had accepted and was nervous that he had made a huge mistake. What!!!a gift horse!!!literally!!!!!I was over the moon! I still am.

He thinks things are going too fast and that I'm going to give up on the farm and leave him with all these animals once I am bored with it all. He doesn't realise that this is my home, my choice and also my dream. I want a farm I want to work hard, I want to sweat but he being a macho pessimist doesn't understand that, but he'll see soon enough.

Not religious but feel I need to give thanks before going to bed tonight.

The horses arrive in two days! Thank you whomever is behind all this good fortune, may I have the skill strength and intelligence to use it well.

Day 23

Feel like utter pooh!

How can the tide change so fast!!!!I was riding the waves of fabulousness yesterday, and today all the sea has turned to shit.

My long distance relationship, with a man I know is not right but none the less have feeling for, and have been told(by him) cares for me. The animals promised. The horses were taken by someone else for some reason. We didn't accept early enough. But I only found out yesterday! How is that possible. Anyway, there will be others. I hope

Mr N.S.R. told me in a little too much detail that he has fallen for a French girl. He has actually gotten her pregnant!!!What??? Is this really happening? How did it go from, 'when you get here I will make you fall in love with me', to 'sorry babe I got another bird pregnant and want to be with her!' I am having trouble taking this all in, not sure if I am upset or angry! Or even relieved?

"The cowboy" is really upset about the horses. He has an easy way of dealing with this. Two women came over, one a bubbly mum of two, we met last week, the other is a woman she is trying to set "The cowboy" up with. Flirting and flattering the ego always helps.

I hate feeling fragile, let down and a little stupid. I know I had tried persuading myself that there was no future, and there probably never was. Honestly it's a shock to go from someone promising they'll make you love them and then three days later saying they've met someone. The human heart really is a fickle muscle.

I feel quite shocked at my fairly passive reaction though. I am decorating, putting the presents under the tree and listening to carols. I am however going to get the axe out and chop another tree to release my, seemingly non-existent rage. I'm sure there's some hidden somewhere.

Oh and clearly I phoned Shovel hands to ask if he wanted to come over tonight (waste no time do you!). Flirting and flattering the ego mends a heart faster!

Chopping a tree down with an axe!!!!Yipeeeeeeeeeeeee it really releases stress. I love it! Feel invigorated, and tired enough to go to sleep without dwelling on things too much.

Day 22

Got up early to watch cartoons, went to bed early and was called at midnight, as usual fell over, missed the call but just to add insult to injury (actually injury to injury) I decided to put the logs on the fire back in place in the dark. I scorched my hand and spent hours secretly wondering whether it had Mr N.S.R. who had called. If it was maybe he had changed his mind, maybe it was all a big misunderstanding. Maybe, maybe, but NO

It was my brother, who called again this afternoon to let me know he was coming out for Easter. Nice! a bit of company from someone who is pretty good at D.I.Y! Should cheer me up!

I went for a long walk, to fetch the post,(the postman won't come down the 1.5k drive due to the terrible state of it) in the hope of bumping into a neighbour. Not a hope in hell, not a soul in sight other than three hunters going past in a car with a trailer. They were, no doubt, picking up whatever poor creature I had heard screeching in the woods. I really hope that they haven't scared all the boars away (or killed them all), I'm looking forward to making wild boar sausages! I met no-one, will have to content myself with my own company, and stay positive.

I have decided a creative project will help my mood. So I also begun learning a new piece on the guitar. "the cowboy" has shown me an American way of writing guitar music which is much easier. tab!!It's meant for me!! I will however learn to read music again as I am determined to pick up the sax again seeing as I have it here. It is also the sexiest instrument on the planet! Anyway musical projects will lift my spirits I'm sure!!

My lovely Art phoned this evening, he is enjoying London and has plenty of pals, he doesn't seem in much of a rush to see me though, also I suppose the thought of being lost in the countryside in the cold isn't too appealing. The last time he was here there was neither heating or hot water, bit of a shock for a city dweller used to the comforts of modern technology.

I am fairly sure that I have poisoned myself, not only did I go out to pick mushrooms but (I am for some insane reason) forcing myself to drink very ancient Pernot, which smells of turpentine mixed with mint liqueur. Haven't had a drink in a while but this news makes me want to drown my sorrow in anything I can find. Finding, a very old glass bottle, which says dilute 100to 1, so seriously strong stuff! Way out of date of course, looks like the label dates back to the 50's. It's rather nice if you hold your noes when swallowing, due to the smell. Well actually its drinkable(ish), and if it kills me then who gives a shit anyway!

I don't feel unessential to anyone
yet my friends are essential to me
Where has my heart and soul gone
How will I ever be free?
Have I done things wrong every time?
Why can I not give myself
My freedom and love is mine
to give yet I chose to reject.
Where has my heart gone?
Have I a soul
Why are the pieces of broken me
not repairing nor filling this hole?
Will I be dissatisfied forever?

Day 23

Not a very interesting day, not that any other has been you may say. I am still in shock but determined to get on with things as I will be alone doing this from now on. No boyfriend coming to join me, no partner offering to help build our dream home together. AGH! no one just me!!!!

I can do this, I don't need anyone else!!! I don't need a man! I just need myself!!! Believe this!!! Try to!!! Believe it hard!

Went to town to do some shopping. Got loads of winter seeds in the hope that it really makes no difference if they say plant February and it's only December. (Fingers crossed). Went to the café on the square as usual and one of my pals is garçon there. He is great fun and a genuinely nice guy. We had a very brief fling six years ago and I really only have vague memories of it. None the less it was great to see him and I found out from "The cowboy" that he has just started a sheep farm, and does the waiting tables on the side until things pick up. He was telling me all about the joys of having animals!

I hope I'll see him again soon as I can ask him load of questions and also maybe be invited to the carnival as he is taking part!!!Yeah positive things

I also found out today that there are actually quite a few people who live in our tiny village and some are not ancient! Hoping to make some friends and have some girly chats or at least get to know younger people than or anyone other than 'The cowboy'.

Day 24

No way of getting up today! Have no idea why, maybe the cold or the damp, and a warm bed is always hard to get out of, even alone. I am more and more aware of the fact that it may stay very lonely in this bed! The sadness is also making it hard to want to do anything at all! But this place will be amazing in a year, so stay positive Tabby!!!!

Day 26(6crossed out)7

I really am a complete tit. (need a bigger bra! hahhaha stupid joke).

I've put some prawns to defrost in a sieve, but not just any sieve a pink and white plastic sieve and I put it by the fire while I made a phone call. I have come back to a puddle of fishy white and pink plastic! Needless to say not edible unless I suddenly feel suicidal. Other than that no traumas today. Went to an 18 year old's birthday party but we left early as "the cowboy" had invited a lady friend for dinner, he can't cook! This actually is the same lady that came over the other night without her pal is trying to hook them up! Seems to be working. It seemed to be going well when I left them anyway.

Phoned Shovel hands to check he wasn't ignoring me, he was bang smack in the middle of a piss up with JaJa and another pal. They really cheered me up. Even though they were very drunk and a little inarticulate I understood something about the village fete committee. They have asked me to join a committee meeting next week which makes me feel very integrated! Also they want me to attend a New Year's Eve party yippee! Feel a bit less alone, and finding a place in the community.

<u>Day 28</u>

Need a bigger bra again!!!Second night in a row where I have been an absolute tit!!!!What is wrong with me? Where is my brain at? I am sitting here reading through an agricultural book while the fire burns nicely beside me. I have to have a daily ritual of getting the fucker lit so I don't freeze to death in the evening. It is surprisingly cold here. I move slightly away as my leg gets hotter, and hotter and hotter. Why am I getting hotter if moving away from the fire? Oh well never mind keep reading, this is useful educational stuff after all, and essential for the future running of the farm. AH!!! Too fucking hot what's going on??!!! I realise my jeans are actually on fire!!!!!!! Yes, I am on fucking fire. Needless to say I'm fine now but feel a bit sheepish in my new pair of jean half shorts.

Have invited the new woman in "The cowboys" life and her bubbly friend for an early Christmas dinner in a few days' time. I've been wrapping presents and placing them under the tree for the two young girls coming with Mrs Bubbly. It's a nice token, and it also gets the Christmas mood started. I do love seeing the excitement of children unwrapping gifts, even if the gifts are meagre and I hardly know the children.

<u>Day 29</u>

Honestly, I need a bubble wrap bra at this rate!!!

Nearly died today! No really, we took the tractor down the awful drive to the nearest farmer to get 2 bales of hay but found only one. When we got back home we emptied the crap out of the garage and placed the hay against the wall and replaced the crap onto the tractor. "The cowboy" then got me to drive it to the burning pile, this was easy enough even though I have never driven a huge tractor before. I then had to turn round on a slope in the space of a few meters, because the trees and bushes, meant there was very restricted space between burning pie and trees. This could have been simple if the soil had not been so damp from the rain. As I tried to reverse while facing down hill in front of a row of trees the back wheel skidded. At first I just thought I wasn't moving because I'd made a mistake. "The cowboy" jumped off the back to come to my side. He asked me to slowly move forward, he then pressed on the back break and got me to reverse. No luck. He then got me to press on the clutch and let the tractor roll forward, then try reversing again, but my leg was shaking on the clutch so much that we jerked and jerked before he realised that if he didn't take over I was likely to roll down the hill at full pelt straight into the trees.

God knows what day I've lost count.

"The cowboy" thinks he's gonna die, as usual but now he has reason to. He's been told he was lucky to escape a heart attack. Not sure what to do or say about it, so kinda try to stay positive for us both, and carry on with daily chores

Organised the early Christmas dinner, decorated the house with tinsel and glitter, the table was strewn with a white cloth, gold painted pine cones and umpteen candles.

I cooked a traditional turkey, spuds, sprouts, bread sauce, all the trimmings. We had aperitif in the lounge, with fire and tree sparkling as well as champagne. I then did my lady Christmas act and gave everyone a pressie much to their delight and surprise.

I showed the two girls my princess room. It is actually the bed room in the tower which is now purple, silk and glorious. Shmona has privilege of that room when she visits being firstly obsessed with dark and mysterious things including purple and second because she is without doubt my fairy princess!

Dinner went rather well considering Shovel hand's slight shyness especially around strangers, the imminent getting together of "the cowboy" and charming blond lady and lets not forget the mother's endless disappointments, which she shared far too easily with us all. The bubbly lady is being claimed out of house and home by her ex-husband. This did at points kill the conversation but the Christmas spirit flowed like red wine and drowned the gloom. This was a point when Shovel hand's tact surprised me, he knew when to add a cheeky or amusing comment without causing any offence, in fact clearing the air very well! What a pleasant surprise!!

Once the girls had gone to bed I did a test on them all, asking them questions about their likes and dislikes in the aim of analysing their personalities. This was brilliant fun, the mood was relaxed and humorous. After a series of mundane questions, ie what is your favourite drink and why? or what do you think of when I say the word 'water'?. The fun really began when everyone fell into hysterical as "The cowboy's" idea of sex was analysed as "Jesus walks on it!" Really, you couldn't have invented the scenario without a multiple personality and a twisted sense of humanity. I mean how pretentious can you get?!!!

I then read their tarots, which was terrible, as I started with bubbly mum, who's reading was dire to say the least. Shovel hand's on the other hand was apparently very accurate and his future is glorious, with two cases of being told he is to have a fortunate marriage and luck with the opposite sex. We all clearly invited ourselves to the future wedding.

He has changed since I was with him, more relaxed and sure of himself. He is probably still a little too shy but he is a really good friend and I seriously trust him. I am so fortunate to have him near by, and happy for him that he has more self assurance.

Unfortunately my thoughts on "The cowboy" are confusing. He seems to want to protect me and dominate at the same time. This could be his macho masculinity revolting against his age, illness and weakness. He is I have to say very sexist, which I really can't stand, but put up with as I need his help. The problem is that he cares for me less as a daughter than as a potential life companion which is disturbing. In fact it totally repulses me, he is at least 40 years older than me, and sickeningly sexist! 'worried'

I laugh off comments like, 'you are almost the perfect woman', or 'if I was only 20 years younger!' Where do I stand, is he a threat? An employee, friend? Or a burden? I know he thinks we are very similar but we aren't and, when he talks of his wishes and desires in terms of what we both want I find it presumptuous but worse intrusive.

Catherine, the potential new squeeze is a seriously lovely woman but he keeps telling me he's not in love and uses his usual sexist expressions when talking about her. She is intelligent and charming, but has lost a husband and is therefore fragile and vulnerable. She is attractive, and yet 'the cowboy' dares say things like 'she's not that bad for her age', when she is actually younger than him! My worry is that, either he really is a materialistic heartless macho or worse he is trying to tell me it's me he wants. I need to push them together a bit more, but subtlety is primordial.

Today we went to town to take the empty gas bottle back, after the 20 minutes journey to town "the cowboy" realised he had forgotten it at home, great. Considering he is so economical about how many times we go to town(stingy), this was a blow. He was beating himself up about it but I understood he had other things on his mind like his health or the memories of the first night with Catherine. He sadly told me later in passive tones half jokingly that I was confusing his thoughts, and ranted about my abundant qualities. I took it as a joke and laughed it off. What else can I do? I'm a little scared of him so I think it would be unwise to confront him. Not only because it could be meant jokingly but also because he is emotionally unstable at the moment due to his illness. He also has a few guns and a lot of knives. We are quite isolated up here on the hill. Cabin fever

Anyway all that aside, I will be in Spain in two days with my new little nephew and family! Christmas look out!

Don't know what happened but last night once in bed I decided I was really not tired. I went down to play music and danced like a maniac in my bra and pants till three in the morning. Flicking the lights on and off to pretend I was in a disco:!!!Yes I am that sad!!!

I went for a two and a half hour walk today, to a small village down in the valley. It is much like our village but some of the houses are so well decorated and the gardens are well kept that I believe there could be some interesting acquaintances to be made. I only saw three cats and one white van but I am sure there is life here. Please let there be some fun and friendly people around.

I found that the leeks and the onions I have planted two months early are growing, joy!I planted them in small pots in the kitchen so that they would not freeze, near the window so they also get light. So I went to collect more horse shit, planted carrots and celery then constructed a device to keep the heat in with rope and bubble wrap. A kind of makeshift green house if you want. By the time I get back from Spain I may have a veg garden in full growth in the kitchen!

My guitar playing has improved and my German is slowly but steadily increasing. My general education in other words is advancing as are my plans. Even though I'm terrified of bumping into Mr N.S.R', I feel confident about going to Spain for the week, to party, go manic, and revive my family contacts before setting to work on driving licenses, jobs, goats and general advancement in life.

The plans for my Ant's 50th in February are going well too. Have called a few old friends in Scotland to see if they can come to Spain. Have booked a bar and will be doing the catering with my cousin. Also, my aunt has a strange obsession with monks, so we have booked a stripper dressed as a monk. What a great surprise. She'll love it!!

Spain!!!

Am now in Spain, change pen! (This one is too finally running out, and just not Spanish enough).

Have now left Spain, and was so busy I forgot to write. The joy of seeing my sister's new born boy, the sea, sun and all the rest of the family and Christmas spirit was overwhelming.

My sister and I dutifully filled stockings and hid them under her bed along with all the presents. The flat was neatly decorated with tinsel, stars and an array of chocolates and sweets in glittering bowls. I brought the c.d of Christmas carols, I had been listening to at home, with me so that she could hear English carols like we used to with my mother while decorating. Traditions and fond memories make Christmas the contradictory emotional roller-coaster that it is. It fills me with love and nostalgia all at once, tears of joy and sadness all at once.

Daily routine in Spain

I walked down to where my aunt works most mornings for coffee and a chat. She is a great comfort to me, as I said she reminds me of my mother, and so close to Christmas I seem to be missing her more and more. I ritually did the same in the afternoons accompanied by my cousin. Then on day three the inevitable event happened!!! Guess who came into the bar? This is where I bumped into Mr N.S.R.. He didn't stay long said "hello" and one or two pleasantries and left. It was a total anti-climax. He looked thin, old and tired and I felt very little when I saw him but none the less, was smiley and not too overly nice. Strange that such a build up can amount to nothing when taken into perspective. I literally felt nothing! What a relief! I could now move on once home, and get on with chores with my mind unhindered by sex or illusionary emotions.

My sister's husband was on holiday, and this was the first time I had seen him so relaxed. After having run a bar/restaurant on the sea front he was now at home physically and mentally. The hole family atmosphere was so relaxing.

His family, consisting of mum, dad, sister and her awful husband form Paris where arriving just before Christmas and his brother who lives in Spain and is a younger and slightly funnier version of himself would join us Christmas Eve for dinner.

This Christmas eve dinner, was held in a lovely old house near the mountains, with a stunning view of the sea and the sun setting over the blue and purple water.

My sister and I brought stockings for everyone, so that they would wake Christmas morning with their respective gifts and would be entertained till the present opening after lunch. The tradition in France is to open everything in the morning, or even straight after midnight, but where's the fun and anticipation in that? The torture????hhahahah

I woke early Christmas morning with my niece in the bed next to me, whom I thought would be rummaging through her stoking already. No luck, she wouldn't wake, I coughed loudly and even threw a teddy bear at her in vain. I can't be the first to open my stocking! They will find me so childish!! So I trundled through to the kitchen to prepare breakfast for sis and hubby. Realising it really was too early to wake them I ventured back to my room and woke my niece with a baby bottle full of hot chocolate.

I sat on my bed and opened my stocking while she adjusted to involuntarily being awake!

She finally took in what I was doing and wanted to climb into my bed to open my stocking with me. I showed her that there was a similar object on the end of her bed but it took some persuasion to get her to realise it was for her and full of pressies too. She is still only three after all.

The first gift was slowly pulled out arduously. With one hand glued to the baby bottle that was in her mouth the process was hard to watch, but we were both very patient. There was no way she was going to let go of her hot chocolate, even to have two free hands for unwrapping. She was still half asleep, her blond curls were windswept and sticking up like an antenna at the back. Her bright blue eyes slightly glazed. None the less, the small plastic sphere containing a wind up penguin was extracted form a well stuffed sock, and joyful exclamations began "pegin, pegin, look Tabby!" She played with the penguin for at least ten minutes before I could take the strain no longer! There's a whole stocking full of other things, more goodies!! But she was happy enough with pegin! (How times change)

In all it took nearly two hours for her to open all of her stocking in which time I made breakfast for everyone, and a vat of coffee. Once breakfast ready, I took a tray through to sis and hubby as well as their eager daughter and we all four sat opening stockings oohing and wowing while having a lovely breakfast of coffee, chocolate and hot croissants. Screeches of pleasure erupting from the small child next to me every time a new gift was unravelled. This opening ceremony took a little less time, and we all then got showered dressed and ready for the day. And new baby was fed and washed too, in preparation for his first Christmas ever.

Preparation for Christmas lunch then began with a bottle of bubbly for sustenance. Our cousin arrived first so I joined her for coffee at her mother's bar for a few minutes before the guests all arrived. My aunt was in good spirits and I decided to give her one of her gifts as she would not be able to join us until much later.

When the family arrived for lunch the flat seemed packed. The terrace was reserved for us smokers and I dashed between there and the kitchen to check on the lunch situation.

The horrible husband from Paris was intrigued by the crackers placed on the side plate of each guest and promptly asked what they were for. We explained the tradition of everyone crossing hands and pulling the crackers all together, and that inside one could usually find a silly hat, pointless gift and terrible joke. The explanation of the cracker pulling during the pudding, i.e the end of the meal, was ignored and he proceeded to open one regardless of our cries of complaint. (He is a total arse!)

Lunch went well, long and entertaining with far too much booze and the occasional snide comment from Arse face. I suggested a board game for after lunch, one where language would not be a barrier, and everyone could join in and have fun, but Mr Arseface was not impressed. So the idea of a game was forgotten. Shame, think it would have been a good idea, but usually when people want to impose themselves when out of their depth they seem to have to disagree rather than agree with the general consensus.

Usually present opening is slow and fun but this year it was a frantic race which I didn't enjoy in the least and actually sneaked half my presents off to my room so that I could savour the opening ritual and appreciate each gift in turn.

Anyway the events rolled on rather quickly and ended with my aunt turning up, me doing charades and my sister and husband wishing we would all piss off so that they could go to bed!

I was unfortunately completely hammered and finished the night with my head in the toilet, which I was quite embarrassed about, but forgiven for by my sister.(it's Christmas after all)

Boxing day, terrible news!!!! Tsunami!!!Thailand! Our cousins are there! My godfather and his family. We were getting regular reports from his brother, but the reports were not great. The wave had crashed into the house and swept the whole family into the sea. My godfather had managed to get them all to safety one by one. When he was sure they where all safe he then went out to help other victims.

There was no news, no news, still no news. No-one knew where he was.

And then a day later!His own son found his body, his feet sticking out of the mud!!!Shock, sadness, empathy and so any tears.

All the few days later were spent in a haze, playing with toys and recovering from hangovers until my ominous departure. The thought of being alone after such a busy week was terrifying, the fear of depression creeping up on me was doubtless in my mind. I none the less, bit my lip, held my head high and headed for the bus home, tears welling but held back.

Clearly, coming back to this house is always an adventure. "The Cowboy" informed me as I was on my way that he couldn't actually get out of the drive to pick me up because if the snow. What snow?? My bus arrived at 5.30am 45 minutes drive from the house. I knew no taxi numbers and was terrified of asking someone such a favour.

I eventually saw no other way, I phoned Shovel Hands who kindly said he would pick me up, but that there was no snow where he lived only 20 minutes from mine. I therefore did not believe that The Cowboy could not pick me up, he just wanted to show me how much I needed him and is car! Yes, I really need a licence in this remote place. But at least I am no longer heart broken!!!Yipee. The climate is unpredictable up the mountain at the house and utterly different to that in town. I did not yet know this.

Shovel Hands arrived as promised but my bus was nearly two hours late, I believe he could of gladly rung my neck. He had been waiting since 5,45, but I had no battery left on my phone, so couldn't warn him. As we drove home I had images of a white village and me out snow boarding in the garden, but no, no snow not a flipping flake. As we drove up the hill there were signs that there had been snow but I was mortally ashamed. Not only had he come to pick me up at dawn, I had been two hours late, and the claims that the driveway was blocked by snow looked like a myth.

"The cowboy" just didn't want to get up so early, what a cheek! Then thud! We stopped dead at the end of the driveway in almost two meters of snow! How can there be so much snow when there is not a flake in the village, less than 3 kilometres away!!??

The wind had blown it off the fields onto the road, and the trees on the other side made a barrier so the snow just accumulated into the road and off the fields. Proper snow drifts!!!.

So Shovel Hands left me there, as the sun rose on the glittering snow I waded a kilometre to the house to get a sledge. I waded back through the snow to the end of the drive, the pink glow glistening off the ice blue snowdrifts, and dragged my suitcase back down to the house for half an hour. It kept falling off the bloody sledge, and I had not thought to bring a rope.

It was dramatic, beautiful, painfully cold and tiring and totally comical all at once.

A few days later I am now preparing for new year in the village. We are to be over 100 people in a small garage, eating a five course meal served by JaJa, me and other helpers.

Am a little sceptical about how so many people will fit, this also perplexed the others who spent most of the first day of preparation deciding where to put the tables, but also decorations as there are a few comedians who like ripping things off the walls.

The night came and we were running around like blue arsed flies, serving drinks, food and being polite to very demanding and more and more inebriated partyers. I don't remember much after midnight, by three I was plastered from having mixed so many different drinks with a lot of help from the boys. I was taken home at 7am and crashed out, only to be woken a few hours later by JaJa and company to clear the nights mess and party a little more. Agh!!!!!I am so tired!!!Help!!

I was dead to the world, the cold I had been tending to since my 5am arrival in the snow had hit its peak!

The fact that my godfather lost his life in the Tsunami in Thailand, a few days previous didn't add to my recovery. A mix a fatigue, sadness and low immune meant I was getting iller by the second.

My godfather's death was a shock that just made me more vulnerable to the virus it I think.

He was a kind, generous, unique man, who worked helping others all his life, and ironically lost his while helping others to safety. He worked for a charity out in Nepal, and used to travel with his family to a holiday house in Thailand, on the beach. I kept thinking of how, when the wave hit, the house was swept of all inhabitants, my godfather helped his family to safety at the top of a mountain, where they would be safe from the aggressive walls of water. He then went out to help more victims. He could have stayed safely with them. Life and death is a very cruel thing at times. Do we ultimately have any control of how we lead our lives and when it can be taken from us. Should we wait until its too late to make the most of it! On that note I want to say life is a precious thing make the most of it. No matter how good you are to others destiny will come, life can be lost for no reason in seconds.

Going to London to see my solicitors, generally about my godfather but also to see Margarette, who is my godmother (not related to godfather).She kindly offered for me to come and stay for a few days of comfort, company and love. She was so right as I have a cold and was getting rather miserable.

Busy, busy time, saw far too many people in too many different places in so little time to go into detail. Saw Art and decided that he is too much of a control freak and has plans for life far too strict for me. Saw Aussie (that I met on the night bus) but only for seconds. Saw my Oxford pal who seems to get more interesting and lovelier every time I see him, and finally big boobs, my best friend from school, whom I went travelling with to Thailand with last year. She is fab, a complete tart with big brown eyes always lined in thick black liner, and big boobs hence the nick name. I had a great time all in all and managed to restrain myself in the January sales.

Again! Coming back is always an eventful process! Torrential rain, when "The cowboy" claims it has not rained and has even been warm since I left.

Before leaving, I had cleaned the house top to toe so that I wouldn't come home to mould or cockroaches. No such luck! I came home to a horror film. It was evening, so 'The Cowboy' went straight home. The kitchen was swarming with huge black flies, coming out from cracks in the window, doors and flying all around my head. I means thousands of them, just terrifying. I nearly vomited a huge scream of terror.

What an earth had happened? How had he not realised, is he trying to scare me? Is he just so macho that it's not his job to clean my kitchen(which had incidentally been clean)?

I now know what this nightmare was due to. I had not cleaned away all the small pieces of burned rice, which had appeared somehow ll over the kitchen. The small burnt rice grains that I believe to be eggs, were clearly dung fly eggs!

How did they get there you may well ask and why did they hatch? The onions and carrots that I had pot planted indoors had cow dung on them. Due to the heat indoors and the weather they had hatched explaining why they were only in the kitchen.

Luckily before leaving I had also put all the plants outside, if I hadn't I don't even want to imagine what I would have come back to! The problem needless to say was cleared through killer spray and yet again a lack of heating! Yes my petrol has run out and I have no heating but I do have a new puppy to keep me warm.

Boadicia, who is currently named Sweetie, as it suits her much better, was given to me by my neighbours. She is such a comfort, and it's great to see her evolve so quickly.

Boadicia is about two months old, just on solid food (don't need another bottle fed animal). She was terrified and hid under the table for the first two days. She now wines every time I leave the room, is almost potty trained and has set times for bed and wake up; all in three days! God I love her!!!

I get up at 4am to play a little and by 8am I have to be down stairs. At night she wines to get upstairs and gazes pleadingly with her hazel eyes until I go to bed! She's maybe got too much control I feel she might be wrapping my round her little paw.

Run out of hot water again! This is costing more than I expected but the weather is now much better, the sun is shining, the hundred mile hour winds have stopped and I can finally tend to the garden.

Have phoned Bruno who will sell me some vines and is going to let me know if I have the fit spot, how deep to plant and hopefully give me a hand.

Have been writing my valentines cards? Sounds terrible but actually it always nice to receive a card even from someone who's not a secret admirer, or even an admirer at all. I just want to let people know that they mean a lot to me but secretly hope I'll receive one myself. Have written a note and signed each one so no one thinks that I have ulterior motives and repressed desires. Sent two to Shmona as she is really the most special of beings and probably the one who needs to be reminded of this the most.

Have 40 days until people start arriving for Easter, so I am motivated to make the place look great and try to have a proper productive daily routine till then.40 days may seem far away, but it's good motivation, and reminds me of Jesus!

Have to start driving lessons, planting the vines and veg, not to mention flowers to make the place look homely. The inside of the house will also be a chore as each room, as I've redecorated has been emptied of shit which needs to get sorted and go somewhere. It's been moved from room to room but in 40 days every room will be in use and therefore needs to be emptied of said shit.

In other words, the next few months are going to be busy, the goats are due in almost a month too! So milking, feeding, cheese making and any other unexpected chore that needs doing! <u>What fun!EXCITING</u>

Look like a right house wife today other than the huge combat jeans with orange and yellow zips. I have had to put conditioner in my hair and wrap it in a scarf for a day as I can't get a brush through it, and it's too damned cold to have a cold shower! Still no hot water. Just to make matters worse I'm sure the bloody goats have generously given me a few tick bites, from the ticks living in their fur. Sharing is caring but there is a limit! The prospect of having a cold shower tomorrow to get it all out is not very appealing as the house is a bit chilly at the moment what with there being no heating either. But yes tomorrow wash conditioner out of hair!

Bruno is coming round tomorrow to tell me where and when to plant the vines he is selling me. Will be nice to see him again after having made such a tit of myself at the village New Years party. Might even get him to stay and watch the rugby with me.

One of the only sports I will watch, 6 nations.

Seeing Bruno was great, actually it really got me in a good mood. He was very enthusiastic about my little farm, and plans for vines. He has agreed to sell me 60 plants and will not only give me a very reduced price, but has promised that the post sale services will be ongoing. This means that he will help me with each stage of the viticulture process! We had an aperitif and talked of future projects, perfect partners and agriculture. We get on brilliantly but there is always a slight awkwardness because he is shy and clearly still has some feelings for me though I am not sure which. He is used to the old impulsive me so I probably confuse him.

After he left it began hailing! Then wind, then snow, the electricity cut out for a few minutes and I can only imagine that there is someone having a right laugh at me up there. Go on throw all you can at me, I can take it (I hope).

Woke this morning with only a small amount of hail and ice on the ground but the snow started at 8am and hasn't really stopped since! We are stuck in again! For at least four days but this time I have no hot water, no heating and three logs left! Panic!

Went out dressed for the north pole, to the woods to collect wood with the howling wind and snow trying to dishearten me, in vain I'm pleased to say. I am now next to a toasty fire, with the pup chewing on a branch and feel ready to face tomorrows challenges! How can I get a garden started if there is this much snow? How do I wash the conditioner out of my hair, how do I get to the shops, all these questions are insignificant when the only thing you can think about is how do I not freeze to death!!!!

(Clink) cheers.

Real Fear
Real freaking frantic frustration
How to survive?
Why has my feeling gone? Will I ever get home?
Cold soul cold heart cold,
Just cold upon cold freezing me up
Ice in my heart and ice on my hand,
The warming light has gone out
The supportive candle is blown away
creeping closer, in the dark, lurking
growing stronger at my side, invading
Shading the sun from my path
Fear is crashing in like a storm
I just want to be warm!!!!!!!!!!!!!!

Still stuck, even though the snow plough has been. A neighbour with a tractor gets asked by the council to clear people's roads, with a makeshift metal plate he has screwed onto the front of the vehicle. He and his son sitting high up in the cabin, arrive in a loud rumble of ploughed snow, stay for a coffee hot chocolate and chat about the other stranded villagers, who can actually get out. The problem with my driveway is that it is lower then the fields on either side, and the wind up here is blizzardy. So a few minutes after my neighbour leaves the snow from the fields is blown straight into the road and creates huge snow drifts.

The snow hasn't stopped so we got "The cowboys" bird to drive us to town, each with a rucksack to do some shopping. We walked back up from the village, in the snow for half an hour, with the light dimming, both quietly loosing our footing and morale while also losing feeling in our hands and toes.

It will be a while before a lorry load of diesel will be able to get here and get the heating going again. I am sat by my meagre fire trying to regain sensation in my hands and toes. Now listening to music, drinking a wee glass of wine and again ready for anything. Tomorrow I will have to head out to the woods to get more wood but the weather is getting warmer, (wishful thinking) still snowing but not freezing. I am dreaming of a hot bath, full of bubbles and the heating on, ready for me to get out of the bath to some warm jimjams which will have been resting on the radiator. I can dream on!!

As the wind howls outside to remind me that I can't do anything about the cold, the lack of wood and the poor pregnant goats slowly running out of food, I put on my woolly socks and ski trousers and chuckle internally at the shear insanity of the situation. I ran to of gas for the cooker today but luckily have another spare. The problem is that it is so cold that the gas is not going through the pipes well, I didn't realise gas could freeze!. It will soon flow properly and anyway I can always cook on the fire, I'll need to get more wood in though.

Had a good cry today, went out with two pairs of tights on, two pairs of socks, two pairs of gloves and sallopettes on to get wood. After ten minutes I was in agony my fingers were frozen! Frost bite is like some elf sticking needles under your skin, into the flesh bellow the nail at the ends of your fingers, where all the nerve endings are! SOSO painful writing it can't even come to a tenth of the pain. The water pipes had frozen and the pipe for the goats water too! I can't take it. Well that's a lie. The things we take for granted like heating, hot water and being able to go shopping are actually not essential. Dreams, hopes, inspiration, creativity and a sense of perspective those are what keeps us going in life! And a damned good sense of humour. But the weather report has announced worse weather coming this weekend. Worse! Can it get worse!!Oh well just try to keep yourself and the animals alive.

Today again, the pipes were frozen, BUT.......... it wasn't snowing!!!!!!!, everything had melted a bit and frozen over the top. I decided to take action. I went to the woods across the horses' field equipped with a sledge and waded through the snow into the forest. The wind was ice cold and yet the sun shone. A reassuring ray of hope in this white wilderness. This patch of wood is where "The cowboy" had been chopping trees and had piles from last year and this. Due to the problems with the tractor we haven't been able to go and collect for this winter, well this was what he had told me anyway. I decided to pile four logs onto the sledge but they were too heavy. The cord broke and even with only two the sledge wouldn't move. Surely a sledge can take a human's weight? Ah, but no they are meant to take a child's weight, and not through woods, softer, easier ground with a slope preferable. I reluctantly returned with one log under one arm and sledge in other. Walking up through the woods was hard, not only because of the extra weight and the cold but the ground was extremely slippery. When I got to the top of the horse's field I placed the log and myself on the sledge and shot like a rocket back to the house. Yup at least that was a fun minute in this horrible ordeal.

"He cowboy" and I made the same trip this afternoon, this time I had two logs over one shoulder. It was hard, tiring and yet I felt totally revitalised by the time we got back to the house. I am now sitting by the fire with the knowledge that this log will last till morning, which means I will be spared the chore of lighting a fire in the morning half awake and shivering and desperate for heat.

Big pat on the back! Not too hard though as it hurts a little.

The snow plough came again today so we attempted to get the car up the drive. The snow drifts were still at least half a meter high and icy, the car swerved and I was totally terrified. After the first icy patch I begged to get out of the car as we had narrowly avoided ending upside down in the field and sliding down the valley to our deaths. We have left the car at the village so that we can get to town in an emergency. I told "The cowboy" to spend the weekend with his girlfriend as he does nothing here but complain, not boosting my morale in any way and she is getting jealous of how much attention he pays to me and the house instead of her.

I tried subtlety to breach the subject of what his role here is but he acted dumb. He really doesn't see me as his boss and has no respect at all, but I am patient....all in good time.

Friday evening I decided to attempt to make bread seeing as I had no freezer(who needs one in this weather!) I had no provisions really and only what I could carry in a small rucksack to keep me going. Flour doesn't go off and is cheap! So I made bread dough once I had managed to melt enough snow to mix with the flour and make dough, with yeast. I left the lot on the fireplace to rise and got back to general dinner prep. Chopping onions and cabbage into a pan with I was going to boil on the fire, while listening to music and sipping a glass of wine. Very civilised, am going to have a quiet calm night in and relax.

I put the pan on fire to boil and check my dough, its ready to transfer to my makeshift oven and be placed on the fire. I take the empty bowl back to the kitchen place it in the sink and pour cold water which I had defrosted earlier, over it to wash the residue dough off.

Crack!!!!!OW!!!!!!What the hell is going on???!!!!!!
Wow blood everywhere? Why what the......
I look down and the bowl has actually exploded! There is blood everywhere, and I can see the bone on the inside of my wrist!!!!!No way what???!!! This is not happening, right stay calm, stay calm, must keep hand high or will lose all my blood, ok ok, try to find white piece of cloth to wrap wound and put pressure on cut. Ok Ok blood all over the

stairs while searching for a bloody piece of white cloth! Why not just any cloth!!!Bloody scout training, always showed us with a white cloth. Right must phone for help! Phoned closest neighbours who said they were on their way, was a long wait so called my sister in Spain so as to stay awake and not pass out, not the best idea in the world, she just got angry at me!I was not aking for herhelp of course she couldn't do anything from Spain, but I needed to stay awake until neighbours arrived. Got off the phone to her as she insisted I get ambulance out!Then the phone rang, phiew, no not phiew. The neighbours coud not get here, the blizzard was too bad, but they had called the ambulance which was on its way. They wanted to know if it was an accident. Why???? Because if I had tried to cut my wrists they would have made less effort to get to me? What??? The neighbour had called neighbours up the road, who had a tractor and actually easier access to the house. It took them and hour to get to me, but when the small tractor arrived with a tiny flash light barely visible in the snow, I was extatic!Saved at last! We chugged up the hill blinded by the snow blowing in all directions, and at the top of the hill, a miracle! Another neighbour of mine in A CAR!!!!How had he gotten up the hill? How was he not upside down in a ditch, who cares! I was rushed from the slow moving tractor to the car, which had to be driven in reverse with the door open to protect us from the snow, but also so that the driver could actually see where he was going as it was utterly pointless to try and use the rear view mirrors.

We got to the village where an ambulance/ fire engine waited with its flashing blue lights the excitement of the village. I clamber in still holding my arm, helped by two firemen. Once settled I take the bandage off, the bleeding has stopped, so I say oh it doesn't look too bad, thinking oh dear, have I just caused all this fuss for a mere gaze? oops

One of the firemen replies 'doesn't look too good either', and proceeds to dress my wound. Luckily at this point I pass out, as I think the journey took well over an hour due to the snow.

Arrival at the emergencies I am sat on a seat in the waiting room, and wait, and wait, and wait. A nurse comes by and sis that they will stitch me back up once bed if free, could I call a neighbour or friend to come and get me. Of course, and thank god I will be home later tonight in case the goats give birth in the cold.

Then when lying on the bed, two doctors above me discussing fingers, tendons, not quite sure of themselves, so I look up at them and tell them that they don't inspire conficence, I am hushed by both explaining that it all looks a little more complicated than at first anticipated, I may have cut the tendon. Ok so sew it up, where's the problem?

By the time they have extablished that I have severed my tendon three quarters, the surgeon has gone home! What?

Ok so can I go home and come back tomorrow?

No, that's very dangerous seeing as the last quarter may snap and they would have to then search up my arm to retrieve it!

I slept well!!!NOT, permanently afraid of breaking the last quarter with any movement I made.

I was to have surgery in the morning between two programed operations, ok but would I be home during daylight hours??

They could not say and I could see I was getting on their nerves.

So on operating table, with doctor injecting electric shocks unde my arm pits to find which nerves and tendons still function, very painful! Vey very painful, one shock after another, then another then another, start laughing hysterically in the attept not to cry, then another surely this is ging to stop soon, no another, ow, can't take any more burst into tears and doctor leaves. Door slamming behind and opening again for another doctor to the proceed to do the same, great in for round two, bracing myself, but no. I'ts over in seconds, and I am ready to be operated on. A big green sheets goes up so that I can't see my arm, and a nurse looks down at me on other side where I have a drip in my hand.

'everything ok?'

'well actually that hurts a bit'

She ignores me and pushes hard down on the drip

'It really does hurt'

She ignores me again, and the suddenly shouts' can I get soe help here please, I've burst the vein, burst the vein'

I have no idea what's going on, one arm open behind a screen, the other stinging in pain, and she looks down at my worried face and says;

'oh god she's gonna start crying again'

I wanted to punch her lights out, but with both hands disabled it was an imaginary punch that I savoured with my eyes closed.

Anyway, surgery finished back in hospital room, and told by the nurse that I have to wait for the all clear from the doctor before I can leave seeing as I have had anaesthetic. I am not only angry at the whole behaviour of the doctors and nurses, but also worried for my animals, so discreetly while there is no-one in the room, I get dressed with my teeth and left arm. I call a neighbour give them the room number and tell them I am free to leave, not true for the doctors but very true for me. I was more than ready to leave!!!

We left the Hospital quietly, drove back to the village, and got to the top of the drive, where of course there where snow drifts, I said I would be fine to walk home. I got home, opened a bottle of wine, absolute agony!!! Any strain even on the other side of my body hurt, just shows every nerve is connected in some way. Lit a fire and settled cosily next to it til bed time.

Clearly last night was not enough!!! Saturday night there was another huge storm, the electricity cut out and the pipes were all frozen. Non the less I was well prepared with candles, a Walkman with loud speakers to muffle the wind and keep my mind off the situation. The poor wee dog was far more terrified than me! Haven't spoken about her for a while, but all through these hard times she was there, by my side, freezing with me, keeping me warm and vice versa. A great little companion, and a comfort in this terrifying situation.

....

The sun is back!! The road is still fairly un drivable and there is no hope in hell that I'll have heating for at least a week! But I can start planting (yippee). Well that's what I thought, sun/ no clouds means no cover at night to keep any daytime heat in. The soil in frozen solid!

The temperature has dropped drastically; the taps don't even turn let alone run water! The freezer has packed in and the dishwasher fuses all the lights, not that I really need it on my own with a dog.

I have had to unplug it during a cycle which means its flooded the kitchen. I am cleaning things in pots by the fire, haven't washed my hair yet and still have no heating, it is now march and I have been psuedo-camping for two months. Needless to say the morale was so low I may have skipped few days of writing and living in general. The cold and bleakness has begun to depress me severely and to top it all one of the goats is looking awfully thin. There was no sign of a miscarriage so for the moment I'm just assuming she isn't showing as much as the others. She is milking so it's not a phantom pregnancy, not that goats have them.

Wow, the sun,!!!!!! No way, the actual warm kind!!!!!!it's warming up now, the road is still blocked, yesterday I had to pull the car out with the tractor, as we got ourselves completely stuck in snow. Today the same happened to Catherine but I have hopes that the weather will soon melt away what is left on the road. I have hopes of planting vegetables soon, of being warm, and washing like a normal human being again.
I HAVE HOPES

I have to seriously get going on the house as we are going to be 15 at Easter and a few rooms are in serious disarray, there is water damage and leeks in the ceilings, a lot of the electrics don't work at all.

'Dear god, let the temperature rise, let the snow fall no more and let a huge lorry full of Gazoil come and set the bloody heating back on again!'

I woke up this morning full well not full, half full of hope, but NO!!!!!!!Don't bloody believe it! It's snowing again and forecast for yet another bloody fucking week! Where is the sunshine, where is justice where's my lorry of fuel!

The snow plough came this morning but according to "The cowboy" we still can't get out. So I took matters into my own hands and determinedly walked up the hill with a shovel, and got rid of the bloody snow. Yes it took hours, but I was not cold by the end of it!!!!!

"The cowboy" came up on the tractor to give me a hand and squish the slush to make the road more drivable. We should be able to get to town tomorrow. Yipee, 'The Shining' moments are over and I can see a warm light at the end of the tunnel.

When we got home I went to check the goats as "The cowboy" said one looked like she was ready to pop. There was not one, not two but three new born kids lying in the hay. How exciting, and a real lift to the general mood! There was blood and afterbirth hanging from the goat's arse and all over the last born. There are two females (which is great, more milk) and a boy. One of the females is black and weak, if we weren't there to coax mum to lick her clean, by putting salt on her back the poor thing would have been rejected. And died obviously. As things go, the family is all well and healthy, but I'll have to bottle feed them, not only because there are three which is unusual but because the mother only has one udder.

Now that the sun is shining, the kids are bleating and the house is tidyish I feel comforted by the thought of the future.

Spit roast is huge and the other goats will also give birth any day now, although I am still sure that one has miscarried, and I will check her tomorrow. If she has, I can start milking her straight away and read up on how to make cheese. Exciting!!!!

The bleak streak has gone and I'm in a warmer frame of mind despite the chill. Oh and I've had a hot shower, got the scarf off my greasy head and now have healthy clean looking hair. The hot water was not procured here, I was kindly offered a shower and trip to town by the owners of the chateaux down the road.'The Cowboy' had told me if I asked hemp from anyone in the village they would make me repay it ten fold, also told me they all hated me. I none the less walked to the Chateaux, and went to meet and greet the new owners, half English half Spanish family with four children. Adorable couple, and as soon as the mother realised I hadn't had a proper wash for months, she instantly rectified the situation!!!

One of the goats had managed to escape this morning, luckily I was up at 7am and it took me about half an hour to coax her back into the enclosure. Checked that the babies were fine, the little black one is looking very weak but alive! Noticed that the other pregnant goat was losing gunk and was clearly going to give birth today at some point. We went quickly to town to get grain and general shopping. We met up with

Catherine in the café much to my dismay. I knew that "The cowboy" and her have little time together but I was really worried about the goat.

She has bad arthritis and finds it hard to walk but none the less when we got home she had also given birth to three little ones. One unfortunately, was still born.

Four of the five kids are now in the woodshed out of the cold with their mummies, along with Spitroast (the lamb) and the poor goat which has definitely miscarried.

We milked the skinny goat and saw that she was on the limit of not milking anymore meaning she had definitely miscarried but luckily we may have got at her in time to ensure she keeps milking.

The fifth little kid is in a box next to me by the fire. She was looking so weak and cold that I have brought her in to bottle feed her, plus her mother knows she is weak and keeps trying to suffocate her.

Puppy is both curious and doubtful, I think a little jealous too. I feel full of joy and maternal love, it is great. They are all so cute and small. Each one has a tuft on their heads of a different colour. The black ones have little white Mohicans and the brown kids have black tufts as well as long black boots. I am now a real farmer, milking, bottle feeding and learning all that there is to know about country life. Joys and pains, should have some Gazoil soon if the weather keeps warming up. This is amazing, massive turn of events!!! Gonna have a makeshift bath in a fish kettle, I feel a little grotty as I am covered in shit, afterbirth, varnish and mud. I have been bottle feeding the black kid, but as she will only eat from her real mother I have been getting up every three hours for the past 5 days, with a torch in the night, and have been forcing the old goat to let her daughter feed. It works occasionally. The bottle feeding sometimes seems to work, and sometimes I just think she is drowning. It's really hard, and I am so tired, but she is getting her strength up, and can nearly stand on her own. She is a lot smaller than her siblings and peers, but she is looking so much stronger than five days ago.

Horrific, really heart breaking actually to hold a baby (of any species) in your arms while against all odds, trying to save its life in vain. The sweet little black female died in my arms this morning as I gave her the baby bottle.

I held her limp head as she drank, seemingly swallowing but every time I lifted her all the milk fell like rain from her mouth. In desperation I kept feeding and holding her head up to make the milk go down but she wouldn't swallow. Frustration, panic and real anguish, As I lay her in her box the milk bubbled from her nostrils and from her lips. There was nothing left to do but let her go quietly. I am so sad!!!!!!!!!! I did all that I could!!!!

I had hoped so much that I could defy nature and save her, I had even thought of name and seen me, her and pup together playing in the garden! Tears of pain ran from my eyes as I took her out to bury her, no-one and nothing to blame other than my stubbornness and sensibility for the pain I was feeling. Nature had run it's course, the small black beauty was destined to die from the start.

The other four are fine, only have one female though so I am keeping a close eye on her as she is clearly the weakest. Sod's law seems to rule over me.

The tractor also needs fixing as a tire burst while we went to get wood. This means taking the enormous wheel to town somehow and also asking the neighbour to deliver the goat's hay as we can't go to pick it up. On the good side I have ordered Gazoil and will be having a hot bubble bath this time Monday.

Decorating day,

Get my mind off the death, and the cold!

I have been decorating the stone step at the bottom of the stairs and the stone bench outside with mosaic to give a bit of colour, and uses up cups and plates I have broken while being here struggling with cut tendons and malfunctioning dishwashers. It's a messy process but the results are great. The slight messiness and dustiness make it look like it's always been there, gives it a kind of rustic authenticity to the whole thing.

Discovery day!!!

I drank my first glass of goat's milk today it was lovely. I have also bought the product that turn it to cheese. So slowly learning the process.

This may sound crazy, but my dog managed to piss on my head as I walked from the kitchen to the dining room. Clearly, she is not supper pup, nor potty trained! After having taken the carpeting off the floorboards plus their layer of glue and seal, the floor was a little porous. Pup peed on the landing, above the passage to the kitchen! The pee went straight through the gaps in the floorboards, rather than being soaked up by the carpet, (resulting in it having to be washed and scrubbed until the smell came out) and landed on my head as I walked under. So I have now bought some sealing wax in order not to get pissed on again.

Jane, lovely lady who let me shower!, from down the road phoned to let me know she could take me to Carcassonne in the morning. She was at the time feeding her three-legged cat. I giggled a little and told her I didn't know she had a three-legged cat, to which she replied, "well someone shot him yesterday and as a result he has had to be amputated." To add insult to injury she had his balls chopped at the same time so that he wouldn't wonder off again. Tough day for him.

Unfortunately I KNOW that it was "The cowboy" who did the shooting as his cat is on heat and he was getting sick of roaming Romeos romping on his car. I feel dreadful and I'm sure Jane suspects! She mentioned it the entire trip out, so I really felt like she knew. He may work for me, but it is not my fault that he shot her cat, tough I really can't help feeling guilty, and very responsible for the actions of this seriously immature old man.

Have shifted Spitroast and the three males from the goats pen to another enclosure. I can now milk the two mummies and have given up on the third as she has hardly any milk. She is very fast on her feet so it's almost impossible to catch her, she is a little younger and less arthritic than the other two. I am beginning to think that the whole, giving me this gift, was a planned evil strategy. They are either old and arthritic, or infertile.

I am getting plenty of milk from the other two even though they only have three boobs between them, and the black one with arthritis keeps walking in the milk bucket and knocking it over, to try and escape.

The weather is incredible; in the space of 4 days the temperature has risen from -5degrees to twenty one!!!! CRAZY I have planted, watered and sunned myself in the process. The house is still a bit of a tip and very dusty from the fire but it is slowly but surely becoming respectable. Ready for 15 guest arriving in 4 days.

WORK

WORK

CLEAN

FIX

WORK WORK;;;;;;;;;;;;;;;;

TADA!!!!!! All ready for fabulous friends and family to come an stay.

The weekend just before everyone arrived for Easter, I was invited to an annual fête to celebrate the produce of the area. A large wine festival involving music, painting, performances and food, but mainly lots and lots of drinking. This clearly involved copious amounts of wine tasting (without the spitting) and dancing. Then preparations for the village fête in my village began. I was given the task of writing the village name from twinkly lights attached to wire mesh which I had left over from the goat's pen. In the process I clearly managed to make a hole in my finger which then got infected and this allowed me to get much appreciation for my hard work. Hahaha

Then the postering task a few days later. We drive about, putting up the advertising for the village fête all over the surrounding villages and in town. It's not really long enough before the event but non the less a yearly ritual to prove that an effort is made, and gives us all an excuse to have a few drinks together.

We set off at 7pm in two teams laden with posters and large pots of glue. We had to attempt somehow to plaster them with a broken broom end which obviously was too big for the bucket of glue. Patrice was my enthusiastic postering partner who half way through decided to stop at a friends for an aperitif.

The poor man was in the middle of dinner, and unexpectedly harassed into serving us each a Pastice. I was mortified but he clearly knew Patrice well as the atmosphere was utterly natural.

German friends we know from childhood, due to their mother being at university in Toulouse with mine, were to arrive this evening between 8 and 9.I had known them for years, we grew up together in a way, they would visit us twice a yer when we were on holiday in France. As far back as I can remember I have known these peope.

My sister, brother and girlfriend, AND§§§§§§Shmona!!!!! had already arrived and helped to get dinner ready for the five new guests. We began aperitif at 7pm expecting guests an hour from then. At half nine when we were all rather merry a call came telling us they would arrive at midnight. This resulted in a five hour aperitif, needless to say when the Germans landed we were all chairlegged!

On the Friday two more Germans arrived twin sister to one with her new husband, and a couple from Toulouse of which the wife was also at university with my mother.

The house was now clean and full of an international gang of ready partiers! The festivities started with the traditional tour of all the neighbour's farms including here, on the Saturday afternoon.

The aim is to go from farm to farm, drink them out of house and home while singing crude songs and asking for donations to contribute to the band for the night's dance.

I had organised a bonfire and huge fire works as an Easter present for my guests so I was pacing myself on the "tour de table," in order not to blow myself to pieces and also feed everyone including animals before heading down to the village.

We roasted marshmallows, while the trees above caught fire. The hose was rushed to the rescue and generally the whole event was greatly appreciated, and a total farse!!.

The night was dancing, singing, drinking and reminiscing. I was given a lecture on, Shovelhands and my relationship by a concerned friend. She told me it was ridiculous that two people who cared so much for one another weren't together. I explained the fact that I did care too much for him to fuck him while drunk and knowing that I wasn't really in love with him didn't want to complicate a lovely friendship we had managed to create.

Easter Sunday Mass, sacred and essential to the village fete weekend, was missed as no-one got up in time, except me obviously as I had to milk the goats and let them out while the place was quiet.

I had been greatly helped the night before. A group of pissed German and French guests armed with torches and buckets helped me milk after the fireworks, that also added to the night's entertainment.

Sunday mornings/lunch "tour de table" or aperitif starts in the village centre and actually takes place round the farms on the other side from the previous day in order to reduce major distance while drink driving. We again cut this short as it was my niece's birthday and I had invited Jane and her husband, their 4 kids and other neighbours with their two girls for a barbecue. I had in anticipation hidden chocolate eggs around the garden in the early morning after milking not realising the sun would be beating down. During lunch, I had the ominous feeling I would be sending the kids off to search for chocolate sauce, rather than solid eggs.

Another four Toulousers joined us out of the blue and we had enough people reunited to persuade them to do a strip the willow (Scottish dancing). Everyone had decided to bring their dogs with them so the whole thing was a mingle of arms legs and paws.

The effect of this dance was that everyone sobered up enough for the evenings "tour de table".

This took place in the village again due to the drink driving hazard. The gathering at one house, then dancing and singing to the next, then the next and so on, all started well but ended in me with a fractured rib and my sister and Shmona having a huge row.

When we all got home for dinner there were threats of taking earlier flights lots of tears and screams and the entire party atmosphere of the house died. My brother and I took the initiative to play music start cooking giving out tasks and got everyone in a better frame of mind. We succeeded to get dinner ready and basically cleared the air.

Only my sister and I went to the dance but it was still fun and we had a great night. When I got back at about 5 am I got the picnic ready for the next day which is held in a field, consists of omelettes and people sharing their home made products. I took the opportunity to get everyone to taste my cheese, agree to buy milk and cheese from me and even got offered another goat. The atmosphere was great, the villagers are fab and I really think that life is here for me!

Since Easter week I have been painting, a painting I was commissioned for a fortieth birthday. Keep making my cheese and await with baited breath the arrival of my vines. My sister and I have agreed that I should sack 'The Cowboy' as he is really not doing much other than making me uncomfortable, and sabotaging my plans. He also spreads rumours about me to the people in town which are pretty disturbing. My sister told him that the family no longer needed his help, seeing as I was now living here, but he basically told her that I wouldn't be able to cope without him! She found nothing better to do than mention inappropriate comments he had made to and about me, great!!!I will be stuck now a month with, not only a weird arrogant macho ex hitman, but now also and angry and hurt macho ex hitman!

"The cowboy" is very slowly moving out. He is full of snide comments and attempting to make me admit I need him here. Which I will never do. Not because I'm stubborn but because I really don't need a negative force here, nor his lies to the neighbours and his inappropriate feelings towards me.

My godmother has sent me her godson down for a week, next week. He will work for me while he stays and relieve some of the strain on my ribs that are still a little weak. I am sceptical of his abilities as he is a London boy and just far too manicured to want to shovel cow dung or build a chicken hut, but hey let's keep an open mind and a bit of company after such a long time alone (except Easter) will do me good. Anyway he is gorgeous so even if he is useless he can always sit in the lounge and look good. At least I won't need new art work. Hahahahah

Waiting and waiting and waiting for 'The Cowboy' to leave. Everything I do is criticised and undermined. He actively cuts plants I have sked him not to while I am not looking! I mean how childish. It's draining, but I know he will go soon, and I also now know that he purposefully did not get wood in this winter, just to push me to breaking point so I would leave! I am slightly proud of myself now, but also a little apprehensive about the future here alone!!!

Waiting, waiting, waiting, waiting no more!!!!!!!FREEDOM!!!!

'The Cowboy' has officially moved out and in with 'the girlfriend'. Feel a bit sorry for her, but actually very selfishly so so happy he is out of my hair!

Have invited the two nearest farmers with their wives, and a friend from Toulouse who needs some time out. She just discovered she is pregnant from a friend of hers about to get back together with his ex. I obviously offered her love, rest and counselling before the other guests arrived. It's terrible to see a friend in distress and know you can do nothing but hug and listen and let the storm ride. She seemed to forget her woes for an evening at least, and managed to laugh a little.

Dinner went brilliantly everyone had a great time and didn't leave till one am by which time I was fairly pissed. My Toulousaine friend who was staying over decided to get out her fire juggling kit, it's great therapeutic movement when you need to forget. This consisted of two chains with wire balls on the ends dipped in petrol. The idea is to light the balls and swing the chains around.

Obviously I had a go, can't not try a new thing out!!!! Got the chains wrapped around my neck, singed my hair and eyelashes, scratched and burnt my face, but at least I had a go.

I am continuing my driving classes, my instructor lives in the next village so he picks me up on the way to work, and I have first class of the day, then find a willing neighbour to bring me home. Classes are going well after a slow start due to my lack of road knowledge in French. I really need to get a car and licence soon.!!!!The plants in the garden are all growing, the veg I planted with my three year old niece over Easter are flourishing as are the flowers and the grass.

Have to cut the grass very soon. It has gotten so long that the mower will not do it. But I have a sturdy strimmer.

"The cowboy" has been back to get rid of his things and has told me that cutting the grass will take me two weeks when it would take him two days. What a wanker!

James, my fellow godsibling, has arrived. I feel so bad about his first night. While having dinner we talked about my puppy and how to train her as she still pees on my head!!!. He said that the French were quite cruel to animals and even eat horses. I went white at this statement! "You know here is just the same as any other meat no more cruelty involved."

I think he cottoned on as he saw my face. (he was eating it then, I thought it would be a first day treat, oops) Have not eaten any since

"You are now!"

"Great I thought it was beef" he responded with enthusiasm, fake or not I will never know, but I was impressed with this diplomatic response.

The mayor's younger son arrived after dinner and we played a board game involving Mexicans, Indians, lots of drink and undressing. By three in the morning I was sitting with two naked, very cute young men (no complaints), but had no idea what I was doing, they probably didn't either.

The next morning I did say to James that it is actually very quiet here and that neighbours don't generally turn up just to get pissed and naked!(not sure he believed me).

We went to town the next day to find him a ticket back to London as he is dying to get home, neighbours are still taking me into town and back but I have passed my theory finally! Which is the hardest part, and seeing as I am so far away from everything I really need a car and licence!!

'The Cowboy'turned up again, got the tractor out and we went to get some more cow dung. Not sure what part of, you no longer live here he didn't get, but actually it was helpful, and he needed the distraction apparently. I need a good stock of dung for the vegetable garden, so we piled the tractor full, with spades, and un piled the tractor onto the veg patch when we got home. Needless to say London boy was not loving it but was extremely polite about the whole process.

We then played scrabble, which I love and can never find anyone to play with. Don't panic, he loves it too, I didn't force him. He won by miles anyway.

Gave my first French lesson today. The two Australians working at the chateaux came up in the afternoon, so James went out to mow the lawn. The couple are hilarious and great fun, and have absolutely no knowledge of French s this is going to be a long slow process, but we are already enjoying it.

Unfortunately while I was teaching the lawn mower stopped working (because I got oil rather than petrol oops). James carried on cutting the grass with the sheep shearing scissors. HHHHHAAAAA, not sure why, did he think I was a dragon, and that if he didn't finish I would burn him alive or cook him like I had the horse meat? Or did he just like a good challenge? I can't believe it! I'm not a slave driver. He was pooped and utterly sunburnt but the grass was sheared.

The class went really well and they will be coming twice a week.

James and I spent the next day clearing out the potting shed, making lists of what tools I had and what I needed to get. We both got sun burnt while playing petanque afterwards, but a little traditional French boules never hurt anyone.

"The Cowboys" has not had time to move his horse, so this is part of the reason he still comes up, he has promised that it will not be long, just the time to get a fence around a field. His horse escaped that night and both James and I are fairly scared of horses. They are a huge pile of scary muscles at least three times the size of us. "He cowboy" had warned me about the event so we got a bucket of grain which James held as I called the horse.

James ended up being chased by not only a huge horse but three goats and a kid. It was terrifyingly hilarious and when we both got over the trauma we were ready for beer and cards. Which he won again as usual.

ASIDE: Ok. I admit it. Yes I slept with the majors son on Monday. But the worst thing is that I can't remember him leaving and am sure I passed out on him. Just mentioning it, as I realise I have not heard from him, and a little worried that I offended him. He is part of the village after all, so I will undoubtedly see him again.

My field has been ploughed and is ready for vine planting!!!! How exciting is that!!! The field I didn't even know belonged to me, and was being used by a local farmer for his cows, without paying any rent!!! It is quite poor soil unfortunately despite having has cows shitting on it for years. Another issue; it was full of rocks. James and I spent a few hours in the blazing sunshine emptying all the rocks into a bucket until we realised he couldn't aim and was chucking them by the side. Was a completely pointless process basically, as the rocks went from the field, back into the field! Hahaha. We made a pile instead as once the bucket was full we could hardly lift it anyway.

I apologise to my godmother and to Shmona's mum

I have in the past ranted at them about human arrogance with regards to animal intelligence. They really have less intelligence than we do, my dog has been barking at her echo for half an hour and driving me mad!HER OWN ECHO!!!

The vines have now come, so we are planting tomorrow, even though it is absolutely boiling hot! We have a few planter guys coming to help, who seem to drink so much at lunch that I have had to do most of the work for them!!Really hard work! I took Sweetie the dog with me, who ran about the field, sniffing and getting cuddles from everyone in the morning, but in the afternoon, as I was doing more work, she was very interested. She watched me dig a metal spike into the ground, grab a vine plant, and before the earth has time to get back in the hole, plunge the plant into the hole. Sweetie clearly unplanted the first one and promptly chewed it to pieces! Bitch. Hhahahaha, anyway a full half an acre of vineyard planted!!!!!wow!!!!!!!!!!!!

Got home that evening absolutely knackered. The cherries were all ripe at once so I have been taking bags full to the kids at the chateaux and have made loads of jams. Far too many cherries for me to deal with in one go, and have no storage space for now. Very original jams, I might add! With the stones still in.

Farming life is starting, James will leave soon, and I will have to look into this thing called wwoofing I have heard about. I do want to be alone, deal with my emotions and pains, but at the same time I need people if I am to run this farm, and actually I am not a total recluse I need some company.

:Almost TWO month has passed since I last wrote in which time a neighbour and I killed spit roast, I am currently making a rug from his fur. He has been barbecued and devoured. Very tasty indeed:

Back a month:

118

A friend of mine from school came with her boyfriend. I haven't seen her since she moved to New Zealand two years ago. It was so great to see her. All three of us worked on cleaning the house, and garden ready for my 24th birthday party. We also managed to fill the pool from the natural water source. Which means it cost nothing, Bonus!!!!But this is a really arduous process, have to syphon the water through a large black pipe, which I have to suck from the tank first.

The couple helped me enormously. Dan (a neighbour) fixed the lawn mower and cut the long overdue grass for me. My school friend cleaned and tidied everything.

We put the TV, new karaoke machine and speakers out in the barbecue area. The couple from the chateaux down the road lent me paraffin lanterns which were put all around the pool and garden. The place looked amazing. First birthday in my new life, have to make some resolutions!!!

Saturday evening came the music played the fire roared and eventually all the guests arrived.

The karaoke went down a treat as did Spitroast. And by the end of the night most people had sung and swum. Some naked but unfortunately my memories of the night are hazy and in fact I have no recollection of what I did between the hours of 3am and 2pm when I finally crashed out.

Since then I have weeded all my vines, and have planted more veg in the hope the bloody goats don't get at it, they have proved to be a bit of a hassle when it comes to staying in enclosed places, and not eating the fruit and veg trees, even though I feed them every day.

Settling into the village calmly;

Been invited to a birthday; a neighbour's 50th at the weekend. She gave me the dog which I love her for, plus I have known her forever. The party was great except that Art came to stay a few days just at this time.

He arrived with a swish car that so didn't impress me. I had waited 45 minutes at the train station worrying about how I was going to get home if he didn't turn up. After 40 minutes I went to the nearest tabac to get a phone card so I could get a lift home. Obviously this is when he arrived. I spotted him looking for me through the glass windows of the train station. He got out his sunglasses on before coming, (sorry) strutting out to greet me. As we got to the car he tried to get the boot to spring open with some remote, to show off. He was totally mortified that it wasn't working (it was hilarious) if he's known I didn't care he would have been fine with it.

He took me out for dinner in Carcassonne cité which was great. We got on great until he said "I remember now why I liked you so much" threat argh! I realised then and now know that he assumed we would get back together and have children just because he turned up after two and a half years of thinking!!

The next day he asked to help around the farm as he watched me working away. I gave him the task of cleaning out the garage full of "The cowboys" stuff. He said that he would hurt himself without proper gloves (which I don't have). So he read books and sunbathed. Fine he is on holiday, but there is no way in hell I can have someone like that living with me and trying to be my partner on the farm!!!

He had only been here when it was cold in the past and there was no way to visit anything as I had no car. He was useless on the farm so, seeing as he had a hire car I suggested we visit a chateaux and gorges as the area is famous for them. It was a beautiful day out!!! We saw lovely sights, and got on fairly well but very platonically. He had driven for nearly 5 hours just before he was about to drive all the way back to Nice at 5am. I thought he could rest but remembered the birthday!!

The chateaux and gorges were lovely, inspiring but tiring and we had my neighbours 50th birthday to go to.

I was very shy, I knew very few people and Art not a soul. Dinner was fab, full of entertaining sketches even her son doing a comedy sketch she loved. She sang and then this tractor arrived at about 10pm with a huge bail of hair on the front fork. A bit of a strange occurrence until we realised it was a gift delivery.

A DISHWASHER.

Ok not what I would want as a gift! But each to their own! And useful.

She was so funny, 'if I ever complained about the dishes I'm sorry, I've never asked for this, thank you so much'.

Pleased! Considering her valentines gift was a bull from her husband who is a cow farmer! Not romantic but practical. She confessed that for her last birthday she got a mower. So she held no hopes of anything special. Hahaha

The party was brilliant, her husband even demanded that I sing some Edith Piaf with her. Art was getting worse for wear and was leaving at 5am. So I clearly stayed until 4.30 so that I wouldn't bump into him after his children and future speech, then slight comments at this dinner. There was a sweet girl sitting opposite me who couldn't have been older than 15 with her nose pierced and covered in make up.

Art said "I bet when you were her age you were just like her! You know how I want to have kids"

Oh god what's coming next?

"I want two girls and a boy and I want the girls to be just like her." I.e me! I just grinned and downed my glass at his obviously unsubtlety. I'm sorry but if after 2.5 years he thinks he can make me his wife and mother of his kids he's wrong. I thought he'd gotten the message from the way I was with him while he was here.

I didn't get home until 4.30 when he was leaving at 5. So that I didn't see him to say goodbye. It seemed like a good idea but I also took him breakfast in bed so counteracted the late night, I felt too guilty. Anyway I was not as nice as I could have been and feel shit but it was to get rid of a guy who has been planning to make me his wife for the last 2 years, and has nothing in common with me. This is a bit weird if you ask me.

Anyway all is well, he left, I left a note for him to say thanks for visiting etc.

There was my first fête committee meeting which I suggested we have at my place. Bad idea, I was meant to pass my driving test the next day.

JJ, Casanova and wives and girlfriends came as well as the mayor's son that I hadn't seen since last time. He didn't leave 'til 5 am as we had a drinking game with a poor local 18year old who was not ready for this kind of night.

We played some stupid drinking game with dice, went swimming almost naked and eventually the poor kid spewed in the garden as apparently a lot of previous guests but I never knew.

I now have a new wwoofer at last a willing worker on organic farms. He's great, very English and unfortunately for him very white and bald. It is very hot at the moment so he has been a bit burnt! I've offered after sun but he says he doesn't use it? He's done some great work, cutting back all the over ground trees on the road, and weeding the vegetables. It has inspired me to work like a trogon.

The two Aussie workers at the chateaux are now making full sentences in French!!!!Yipeee. They have 2 friends staying with me, the girl has been cleaning "The cowboys" old house. I need a regular income and am planning on renting this three bedroomed cottage out, but it need a really good clean, new electrics and plumbing, but I think a good investment in the end.

She is totally freaking out! She has washed the walls while thinking there were bloody hand marks all over them. Plus the bathroom is still a brown colour after 3 coats of white paint! She has found bullet holes in the walls, and children's underwear in a spare room! Poor thing, I reassured her and said the bloody browness was not dried blood but dried tobacco smoke, she was still not reassured by the bullet holes, but nor was I to be honest.

Although the vines have been chewed by the goats on several occasions they seem to be growing fine. The white wwoofer is working very hard and is the only person to have the guts to tell me I drink too much and am obviously unhappy about something in life. Not sure that helps, but I clearly don't hide it as well as I first thought.

It's not funny when it happens to you
There's no objective point of view
All the past judgements you propose
About the others seem so close
So wrong, why did it take so long?

How to act? React now?
When individuality is lost,
It did happen, but how?
When you avoided it at all cost

No complications in your eyes
I see your heart watching mine
Teaching me for the first time
What I have lost is my own lies.

He did actually make me cry by telling me that real friends tell you like it is and don't just let you bury yourself in drink and solitude. He doesn't realise what I was like but he has a point. The truth is always harder to take than false kindness. I respect him for being so open and honest although clearly he has a very restricted view of me as he doesn't know me.

He has told me that I treat everyone the same and play an act that I am open when all the time hiding my true feelings and fears.

Yes I am sensitive, insecure and troubled but I am also, honest and friendly and hope people do care about me for who I am not for sex or any other material property.

Yes I am full of contradictions!!! Who isn't???

It is true that I don't let anyone in to my life, really and truly but at the moment I am not ready and too ashamed of the person I feel I am. I am weak and full of faults which most people don't notice as they are gone too soon or react to me the way I hope and try to make them. I have an awful conflict within me. I want to be cared for by someone who will know me truly but I am not entirely truthful. I want to be looked after and left to do whatever I want at the same time. I am so full of contradictions that I even find myself arguing with myself and even telling myself to shut up, which I only do after telling myself I am mad for talking to myself let alone arguing!

I went to the doctors today with the neighbour who turned 50 last week. I was expecting to get my pinky cut off but I have been put on antibiotics, have to get a tetanus jab and will eventually get the infection burnt off. While ploughing the garden I got a rose thorn in my finger, I obviously didn't get it all out, and it get very infected, it has actually turned into a small brain the size of a pistachio nut on my finger, that bleeds all the time, though it doesn't hurt. Seeing as I still have no medical cover the neighbour paid for it all, which is then reimbursed. Really good to know there are people I can count on here

She reminds me a lot of my aunt and have a terrible craving to adopt her as a surrogate mother. I don't think she would mind that much but seeing as I have no trust in anyone I start to care about, it my be difficult.

She has invited me to join her choir group, sings beautifully, has chickens and rabbits (which I want to get) and is quite a strong character which I respect a lot. Very helpful to have such a good example near me. Think I will join the choir even though they are all about fifty years older then me.

Seeing as I am beginning to realise my lonely situation, I have to make a concerted effort to go out meet people, visit friends when I can in England, join groups and invite people over regularly, otherwise I will go mad.

Since having workers here my dream seems more achievable. There is so much still to be done but it goes so much faster at two or three rather than solo. Things are finally on routine, an I can see the future brighter and clearer.

Off to Spain for a weeks break, see the family and ex. Decided to spend the extra 10 euros for the comfort of a train rather than the bus.

Spent most of the week in my cousin's bar, not a great idea but better than sitting about doing nothing on the beach.

Managed to convince sis and husband to come to the theme park with me. They had never been together, nor had they been for years! They loved it and I managed to get them on rides they were too afraid to go on in the past, and this was very much appreciated afterwards. A lovely warm sunny break with family to regenerate before starting work again.

Waves of blue waves of green,
sunshine waves all over me
wash my sorrow to where it can't be seen.

Left with a sense of renewal and calm. Looking forward to getting back to work on the farm. Unfortunately the wwoofer I got back to had begun to have serious feelings for me. I dealt with this for about a week until I realised the situation had become awkward and even dangerous. After all I know nothing about this man really and I am alone with in him in the middle of nowhere. I was not sure of the protocol for length of stay or when wwoofers should leave this was my first hosting experience. I now know that most people stay a few weeks, or at the most a couple of months, but that this is actually discussed before they arrive.

I suggested amicably, over dinner, a date for him to leave a month from now, to which he responded "do you want me to leave?"

He had asked me to set a date but clearly wasn't wanting to leave! SILENCE

....

Then the phone rang!!!! Phiew!!!!

I jumped up to answer a phone call, it was two Autrian girls asking if they could come and wwoof in a week's time. I actually asked them how soon they could come, so that I would have an excuse to ask this man to go, I could tell from his face that he was not happy about leaving. He had also told me over the months he was staying that he could not go back to the U.K nor work there, nor would his family talk to him any longer. Obviously I innocently asked him what on earth he had done to deserve such punishment. He told me that if I knew I would throw him out of my house, so I asked no more. I believe everyone deserves a second chance and new beginning as long as they don't abuse of the situation, who was I to judge him after all, maybe I could even help him forward on the next step of his journey.

By the time I returned he had packed his bags!! Apparently he couldn't take anymore of this shit and didn't know where he stood with me! What on earth!!!I was polite civil, and never implied that there was anything more than a healthy working relationship.

Luckily for me the Austrian wwoofers that had applied to come had accepted to come earlier. We went to sleep, him angry, me a little nervous, and then in the middle of the night I heard a van! It may have been a car I am not sure but a vehicle had turned up. Did he know people in the area, or had he gotten a friend to come and pick him up and rob me blind in the process, who was this midnight visitor? I stayed

in bed with all these thoughts flying through my head, until I finally plucked up the courage to head down stairs with the first large heavy object I could find and decided to confront the intruder! It was after all my house, and if I was going to stay here alone I had to learn to defend it. When I got to the front door, shacking in terror there was a face looking through the glass at me, I screamed and then opened the door, only to find it was an old childhood friend popping in on his way back from somewhere, I have never hugged someone so tight. He was a little confused until I explained the situation. We had a chat and a drink and I went off to bed again a lot more settled.

The wwoofer came out of his room as I walked the stairs and asked me what had happened if everything was ok, that was kind of him, I think he is also regretting having gotten so angry.

In the morning when he realised that he had said he was leaving, and had packed his bags ready to go first thing, he apologised. He said his actions were too rash and that he would wait until the work was finished and that I could find some other workers.

He had not realised that I was not going to be treated this way, or continue to feel uncomfortable in my own home. He was a grown man who had made a rash decision to leave in the morning, and that was that! I had made other plans and was actually quite happy to see him go. Still no car so had to ask a neighbour to talk him to the train station. She was not happy with that at all when he saw him. I clearly did not judge him on looks as I just needed the help, but she said he looked like a killer and was very nervous driving him to town, not to ever ask her to do that again! oops

ASIDE: This was my first help experience and since then I have had a continuous stream of interesting and helpful people.

The next couple to arrive were two young Austrian girls, who would stay for two weeks. The day of their arrival was the fête in a neighbouring village, and they had phoned to tell me they had missed their train and wouldn't arrive until late. This became a regular occurrence with visiting wwoofers over the next few years. I was already at a meal in a village when they arrived but I managed to persuade Mr BB to pick them up for me. He was convinced by me explaining how impressed everyone would be at him entering the village with two young foreign girls. He instantly jumped to action drove to town and even stopped somewhere on the way back to buy them a drink!!hahah

Within 10 minutes of their arrival I had them up singing karaoke in front of 200 strangers. The ice breaking evening was showered with wine and local bubbles and accompanied by cheesy men, cheesy music and really cheesy chat up lines.

The next day was a slow starting but I did eventually give them a tour of the house and explained my plans for the next few weeks of their stay. I Showed them how to milk a goat and water the vegetables, weed the vineyard and fix holes in the road.

Within a few days we were playing cards each night and laughing while wheelbarrowing rock loads of gravel up and down the drive way. The road needs redoing dramatically, but is also the only way to the house that won't get snow. Weeks went on, MrBB stayed on to help us, and the general atmosphere was positive and vibrant! Things were getting done, and I had great company too. The girls asked if they could stay on an extra few weeks, to which I did not hesitate a second, we had a lot in common, and work was fun.

I was surprised that we had so many common tastes except one. Paula the most fun and bubbly of the two had developed a soft spot for Mr BB more than twice her age! He insisted that it would be a bad idea to tell me that they were having a fling otherwise I may fling her out. I on the other hand thought she hadn't told me because she was not close enough to me. After all she had only been there a few weeks, and I was her host not a close friend even if we had become great friends in the short time they were here. Anyway after a while I had to make a decision as to whether to leave these two inexperienced girls with my house and animals while I attended my godfathers memorial service in Scotland. I was apprehensive as I had shown them what to do but was still doing most of the daily chores myself. I voiced my concerns, and the two girls reassured me that they were perfectly capable of feeding the goats, and the dog. That they knew how the oven, electrics and locks worked. We also all had phones which meant I could contact them and more importantly they could contact me any time there as a problem.

So I left for Scotland and met my brother and sister, who had also come to honour his memory. The ceremony was more of a big family get together on the top of a hill where my parents where buried than a formal ceremony.

Kind words and malt whiskey passed amongst the group as the usual rainstorm and torrential wind came crashing down. My parent's way of showing us all that they knew we were there for them and truly appreciated the gesture. They added to the electricity already in the air by their own thunder and lightening.

The ceilidh in the evening was far less intense, a lot of drunk farmers in a large wooden hall surrounded by antlers heads and portraits of my ancestors, very few of us were merry enough to really appreciate the scrambled mess of flying Scotsman and pipes, though we did join in a reel or six. A very short but very emotional family gathering, a little less uplifting than the one in Spain a month before. Had to leave the rain and pipes and return to the flourishing farm.

Back at the farm. One goat down and two injured!!!!. Paula and pal hadn't noticed. Something had gotten into the pen and attacked all the goats. A fox or dog, but anyway, what could I do. I had left the house knowing there might be a risk. I was sad about the goat, disappointed that they hadn't noticed that there was one goat less, but I kept my calm, the house was intact, the garden had been tended to, they had been making cheese in my absence, and all in all it's part of the process. They have now left, I am awaiting the next woofers and planning what to work on next in this massive adventure

No boyfriend,
No car
No licence
No caretaker
No idea what's coming next
Nothing to lose.
It's only the beginning.

9 781524 666712